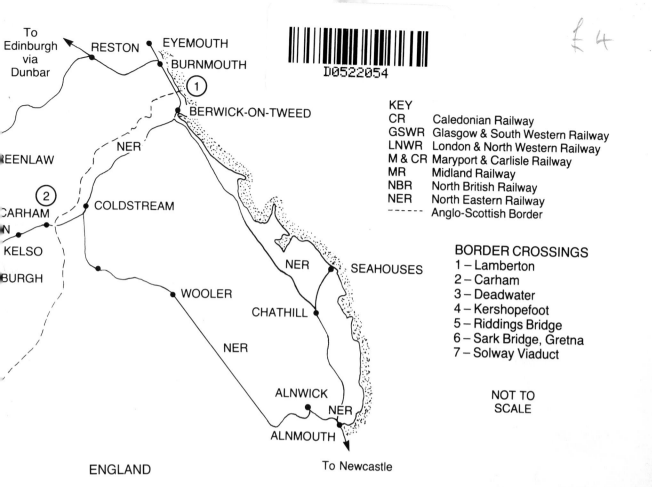

To Edinburgh via Dunbar

RESTON
EYEMOUTH
BURNMOUTH
① 
BERWICK-ON-TWEED

NER

GREENLAW

② 
CARHAM
N
COLDSTREAM
KELSO
BURGH

WOOLER

NER

SEAHOUSES

CHATHILL

NER

ALNWICK
NER
ALNMOUTH

ENGLAND

To Newcastle

D0522054

£4

KEY
CR      Caledonian Railway
GSWR    Glasgow & South Western Railway
LNWR    London & North Western Railway
M & CR  Maryport & Carlisle Railway
MR      Midland Railway
NBR     North British Railway
NER     North Eastern Railway
- - - - Anglo-Scottish Border

BORDER CROSSINGS
1 – Lamberton
2 – Carham
3 – Deadwater
4 – Kershopefoot
5 – Riddings Bridge
6 – Sark Bridge, Gretna
7 – Solway Viaduct

NOT TO SCALE

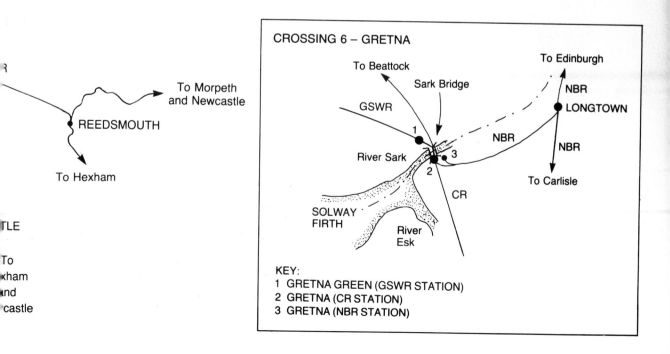

To Morpeth and Newcastle

REEDSMOUTH

To Hexham

TLE

To
xham
and
castle

CROSSING 6 – GRETNA

To Beattock
Sark Bridge
To Edinburgh
NBR
LONGTOWN
GSWR
NBR
1
River Sark
3
NBR
2
NBR
CR
To Carlisle
SOLWAY FIRTH
River Esk

KEY:
1 GRETNA GREEN (GSWR STATION)
2 GRETNA (CR STATION)
3 GRETNA (NBR STATION)

# RAILS ACROSS THE BORDER

# RAILS
# ACROSS THE
# BORDER

## The story of Anglo-Scottish railways

### A. J. MULLAY

PSL
Patrick Stephens Limited

First published in 1990

British Library Cataloguing in Publication Data
Mullay, A. J.
    Rails across the border: the story of Anglo-Scottish railways.
    1. Scotland. Border country. Railway services. Branch lines, history
    2. England. Border country, Railway services. Branch lines, history
    I. Title
    385'.09413'7

    ISBN 1-85260-186-8

Patrick Stephens Limited, part of Thorsons, a division of the Collins Publishing Group, has published authoritative, quality books for enthusiasts for more than twenty years. During that time the company has established a reputation as one of the world's leading publishers of books on aviation, maritime, military, model-making, motor cycling, motoring, motor racing, railway and railway modelling subjects. Readers or authors with suggestions for books they would like to see published are invited to write to: The Editorial Director, Patrick Stephens Limited, Thorsons Publishing Group, Wellingborough, Northants, NN8 2RQ.

**Title page** *Preserved LNER 'Pacific' No 4472* Flying Scotsman *relives her halcyon days between 1928 and 1936 when she crossed the Anglo-Scottish border regularly on the non-stop train whose name she shared. In this picture, the double-tender arrangement is clearly visible as the famous 'A3' heads north past the Border sign at Lamberton on a Newcastle-Edinburgh special on 10 May 1969. (Douglas Hume)*

Patrick Stephens Limited is part of the Thorsons Publishing Group, Wellingborough, Northamptonshire NN8 2RQ, England.

Printed by Butler & Tanner Limited, Frome, Somerset

10  9  8  7  6  5  4  3  2  1

# CONTENTS

# INTRODUCTION

The purpose of this book is to chronicle all seven rail crossings of the Anglo-Scottish border that were built by public companies. Five of these seven are now as much a figment of the past as the Roman roads which traverse the area, and these older transport links are, it must be said, sometimes more visible to the naked eye than the former railways of our own century.

From the cliffs of Berwickshire to the deceptively serene waters of the Solway estuary, seven fascinating railways bound England and Scotland together with bands of iron and steel. This book attempts to show how each one came to be built, the politics behind the choice of route—with at least one disastrous result—and the fate of each closed crossing.

The middle years of actual railway operations are not covered in any detail, partly because the book hopes to appeal to those interested in the modern history of the Borders area as well as railway enthusiasts, and partly because much has been written on the operational side of things already. Exceptions are made where unusual weather conditions have had a major effect on the Border lines—the floods of 1948 on the East Coast and Tweed Valley lines, for example, and the damage to the Solway Viaduct by the ice-floes of 1881. Indeed, the author makes no apology for paying a major amount of attention to the Solway Junction Railway whose history had been little recorded until now.

If this story seems largely to be told from a Scottish angle, this is simply because crossing the border was very much a Scottish preoccupation. Whether or not Dr Johnson was correct in his theory that a Scotsman's finest prospect was the high road to England, it was inevitable that the Scottish business community would want links with the larger markets available in the south; any reciprocal demand was almost non-existent in England apart from Lancashire and from the community of specialized railway investors. Of the seven Border crossings (one of which carried two main lines), four were the direct result of Scottish-inspired construction, and of the remaining three, the construction of which was the product of English railway speculators, two were taken over by Scottish companies, leaving only the Tweed Valley line as an English interloper into Scotland.

There was in fact an *eighth* crossing of the Anglo-Scottish border by rail. This is not considered in the main body of the book as it did not feature a commercial railway built to connect one city or locality with another—the Ministry of Munitions rail network at Gretna was a glorified industrial railway, built without regard to the existence of any such border. Nevertheless, it could boast—although boasting is hardly the correct term to describe the secretive nature of MoD railways—a now vanished bridge across the Anglo-Scottish Border where the River Sark flows into the Solway.

Primary archival sources have been used wherever possible.

# LAMBERTON

## East Coast Main Line

In 1928, Class 'A1' 'Pacific' No 2563 *William Whitelaw* was crossing the Royal Border Bridge at about five o'clock on the afternoon of 15 June. Her crew were working the down 'Flying Scotsman' on its non-stop journey from London (King's Cross) to Edinburgh (Waverley), but they had more to contend with than usual in operating the world's record non-stop train. As well as keeping a watch for signals and observing steam pressure and vacuum gauges, the enginemen were watching for—an aeroplane.

For this date saw an unusual arrangement whereby the London & North Eastern Railway company (LNER) agreed to a suggestion from Imperial Airways to a simultaneous demonstration of air and rail travel between London and Edinburgh. Not a race, of course—at least that was the official idea—although there is no doubt that horsepower was not being spared on either side as the Scottish capital came nearer! But a crucial element in this public relations formula was the Royal Border Bridge which carries the line over the River Tweed at Berwick. It was decided beforehand that the train and plane would rendezvous at the bridge for the benefit of press photographers.

There was an unspoken assumption—and not an entirely unreasonable one—that the Border Bridge actually represented the Anglo-Scottish border, and any perusal of the newspaper cuttings covering the event will fail to locate any mention otherwise. But the fact is that the East Coast Main Line between London and Scotland does *not* cross the Border here. The Tweed and the town on which it stands have been English since the end of the fifteenth century; the present border crossing is some 2½ miles to the north at Lamberton Toll. Perhaps the LNER Publicity Department in 1928 was unaware of this fact; Imperial certainly were in ignorance and the newspapers, hotly championing the airliner, could hardly have cared less anyway.

*One of the Border Crossing signs at Lamberton, north of Berwick-on-Tweed. Erected in 1937, this is the sign on the up side, with the North Sea not far beyond the wall.* (Ian S. Carr)

*The Border sign in the down direction. Below it can be seen the dividing symbol marking the meeting point of the one-time North Eastern and Scottish regions.* (Ian S. Carr)

The railway company did not get round to the simple public relations job of installing a crossing sign at Lamberton until 1937.

As for *William Whitelaw*'s crew and the 'Flying Scotsman', they saw no accompanying aeroplane in the Northumberland skies above the Tweed and pressed on without stopping. None the less, one London picture agency, which had taken the trouble to despatch a photographer to cover this event, produced a superb shot of the express crossing the bridge with an aeroplane only a couple of hundred feet above!

This 'race' was won by the train, no matter what some aeronautical histories may tell you, and was only one incident in the fascinating story of the first railway to cross the Border. As for the Border crossing itself, Lamberton is perched almost on the edge of the sea-cliffs overlooking the North Sea to the north of Berwick. It is almost inaccessible by road and nowadays is passed so quickly by train that the special Border signs are almost indistinguishable.

\*　　\*　　\*

The opening chapter of the story of the North British Railway—the first to connect England with its northern neighbour and historic enemy—began on 8 January 1842. Nineteen Edinburgh citizens met at the office of the Edinburgh & Glasgow Railway to discuss the setting up of a company to build a railway from the Scottish capital to Dunbar, some 30 miles to the east. Within two weeks they had produced a draft prospectus emphasizing 'the probable extension of this line to New Castle'.

A number of meetings followed during the next few weeks, as the promoters corresponded with local aristocratic landowners, made their calculations, and considered the appointment of local surveyors and engineers (in itself unusual—normally English-based engineers were looked on as fairly indispensable for any new railway to be constructed on either side of the Border). On the 19th of the month they took the step of calling their planned enterprise the 'North British Railway', having the previous day resolved to contact the directors of the Great North British Railway to secure 'the purchase of their plans and sections of the line from Edinburgh to Dunbar and also for any information they may also have which would be useful'.

This was a reference to an earlier (1836) attempt to strike eastwards from Edinburgh to Dunbar; the 1842 speculators, despite initially aiming at the East Lothian town, had their eyes discreetly set on what they regarded as a higher destination—the English Border. In fact, the previous enterprise was also visualized as a first step towards the English Border but was virtually 'mothballed' when the government of the day appointed commissioners to consider the future of Anglo-Scottish rail routes.

Interestingly, as late as the spring of 1842 the NBR promoters were nominally still looking only as far east as Dunbar, requiring projected capital of £500,000. However, this was soon to change after the second of a number of visits by the chairman, John Learmonth, south of the Border to assess English reaction to the proposed line. Before the end of the year, Learmonth, a former Lord Provost of Edinburgh, had been voted Chairman of the Edinburgh & Glasgow Railway, largely because of his predecessor's unpopular support for Sunday services on that line; ironically, within a few years an unholy alliance of Scottish Sabbatarians and Lancastrian shareholders was to oust Learmonth from the NBR chairmanship for the same reason.

Learmonth's first trip took him, in the company of two other members of the political-sounding 'provisional committee', to London, Manchester and Normanton, and at the last venue they talked with representatives of the North Midland, Midland Counties, Leeds & Manchester, and York & North Midland companies.

The omens seemed inauspicious. 'Due to the present state of trade', the Edinburgh men were recommended to postpone fundraising activities until August 1842 at the earliest (this was June), when it was hoped that 'the shareholders would get into better spirits', as the NBR Minutes put it. Nothing materialized over the autumn and winter to improve matters, and on a second visit to the south, in April 1843, 'he [Learmonth] was induced to believe that if the parties here [in Edinburgh] were ready to form the line to Berwick, the English parties would be prepared to meet them there, so as to give a continuous line from London to Edinburgh and Glasgow'. The West Coast line—officially 'recommended' by the Government's Smith-Barlow commission (of which more later)—could 'almost be said to be abandoned', claimed the North British supporters.

In the following month, a new name entered the story. George Hudson, the self-styled 'Railway King', began to interest himself in what other speculators might dismiss as a parochial effort to connect Edinburgh with the agricultural areas surrounding it, but instead glimpsed its potential as a link in a chain of railways from the Midlands to the twin cities of central Scotland. In May 1843, Hudson, in his capacity as a chairman of the York & North Midland Railway, informed Learmonth that he would be seeking to extend his line to the Scottish Border, but only if he believed that there would be a line to connect with from the other side (the NBR was still nominally aiming at Dunbar at this time). He also gave Learmonth a useful tip which the Edinburgh man hastened to have accepted by his colleagues. This was the practice of asking contractors to accept a proportion of their agreed payment in shares in the railway company then still unbuilt.

In planning to apply to Parliament for an Act in 1844, and with Hudson's Darlington-Newcastle stretch approved and contracted for, the NBR interests petitioned the Board of Trade with their intentions, particularly in view of the setbacks apparently dogging the 'official' favourites, the West Coast lobby. In July 1843 a Memorial was sent to the Treasury summarizing the hopes and intentions of the

North British businessmen (who were still not a limited company), but which, extraordinarily, received a rebuff from Sir Robert Peel, who predicted government refusal of the scheme. It says much for the optimism of Learmonth and his colleagues that they ignored this, and pressed on with their arrangements. Two 'Superintendents', each with an assistant, were appointed at £4 per week (plus £1 for each assistant) to assess traffic figures, while Engineer John Miller was to 'parcel' the works among suitable contractors, once these were appointed under the new payment arrangements decided upon.

As for crossing the Tweed, there seems to have been an unspoken assumption from the first that this would be undertaken by English interests. In September a meeting was proposed between John Miller and 'any engineer Mr Hudson chose to appoint for the purpose of arranging the point of crossing'. By the end of the month, the NBR's engineer was told that Hudson had asked Robert Stephenson to meet Miller in Berwick as soon as possible. Both Stephensons, father and son, had been asked to give an opinion on the NBR's plans and estimates, and had done so favourably by December.

The autumn of 1843 saw the formal incorporation of a railway to link Edinburgh with the Border town of Berwick-on-Tweed, some 56 miles to the south, its grand-sounding name of *The* North British Railway perhaps a little pretentious in the circumstances. Of course, grandiose company names were very much in vogue at the time; other prospective Border rail crossings were planned for the tracks of the Caledonian, Great Anglo-Caledonian, Central Union, and United Central, to name only four railways, of which three most decidedly would not be built. Two prospectuses for the NBR were issued, on 3 August and 29 November, the company having been constituted at a meeting on 14 November. Its capital was set at £800,000 (later

*In its final year of operation, the 'Queen of Scots' Pullman crosses the Tweed northwards for Edinburgh and Glasgow in the charge of Class '40' No D262, of Haymarket depot, on 30 April 1964.* (Douglas Hume)

*An '03' diesel shunter, No 03 107, waits for the signal to propel two goods vehicles from the down to the up line on the Royal Border Bridge, and then into the goods yard. This historic structure has now changed in appearance with the addition of the electric catenary.* (D. Anderson)

£900,000) in £25 shares, and the subscribers soon included a large cross-section of Edinburgh society and south-east Scotland landowners. It was very much a regional enterprise, with only 42 per cent of its capital subscribed by English-based investors. In contrast, the Edinburgh & Glasgow six years previously had depended on 62 per cent English support; the Caledonian was shortly to rely on no less than 77 per cent of its backing from south of the Border.

With passenger fares postulated at 1½d per mile, annual revenue of £77,985 was predicted for the NBR, including no fewer than 350,000 people travelling between Edinburgh and Portobello. Freight receipts were expected to be some £73,000 annually.

The early history of the North British railway, the first to cross the Border, is too complicated for this volume to go into detail, and unnecessary anyway, in view of the reliable histories already completed by C. Hamilton Ellis and John Thomas, not to mention the excellent centenary booklet by George Dow published in 1946. However, certain mileposts in the history of the line's construction are well worth listing and one of these involves the new company's purchase of the Edinburgh & Dalkeith Railway—doubly important since it also played a seminal role in the building of another cross-Border line, the Waverley Route.

It was obvious from early in 1844 that the E & D management

wished to associate itself with the new, potentially larger, concern planning to link Edinburgh with the south. The E & D had been conceived in 1824 by Lothian coalmasters as an unambitious waggon-way connecting the coalfield south and east of Edinburgh with the capital and its associated ports of Leith and Fisherrow (the latter near Musselburgh, some 5 miles east of Edinburgh). Horses provided the motive power on lines of 4 ft 6 in gauge, the only steampower being a stationary engine to assist trains on the 1 in 30 gradient up to the railway's city terminus at St Leonard's. This site, just off the city's Pleasance, became the centre for the distribution of fuel to Edinburgh's coal-merchants, while train-loads of coal were also taken down to the two ports mentioned from the Dalhousie (Newton-grange) area.

A contemporary description of the St Leonard's tunnel is worth examining, as this feature might have constituted the East Coast Main Line and, although disused, still exists in Edinburgh's Queen's Park, its eastern portal directly beneath the rock formation known imaginatively as 'Samson's Ribs'. In 1840, the railway author Francis Whishaw recorded that the tunnel was 572 yards long, with a 20-foot bore lit by 25 gas lamps. The incline was more than twice as long—1,160 yards—and here horsepower gave way to 'two low-pressure [stationary] condensing engines', with 28-inch cylinders, constructed by Carmichael of Dundee. These drove the cable round an 11-feet diameter drum which would haul up 30-ton loads at a time, totalling between 130 and 190 wagons daily, taking 5 minutes on the journey. The E & D had even perfected 'a self-acting stopper', a device carried on the train to prevent a breakaway on the incline, by the somewhat pyrrhic method of ensuring an immediate derailment.

The E & D was known as the 'Innocent Railway' because of an apocryphal reputation for never having injured anyone. In fact, staff accidents were frequent, as Whishaw records, and C. Hamilton Ellis is probably nearer the mark in ascribing the soubriquet to what one contemporary writer called its 'indestructive character'. At first the company allowed non-company agents to organize passenger services, but took this facility over from about 1836 after discovering that passenger-carrying could be a lucrative activity—earning a revenue of £4,000 in 1832.

However, the E & D 'conductor-guards' encountered difficulties in persuading passengers to buy tickets; members of the public objected to telling 'one speirin' loon' where they were going! In 1839, the line's manager David Rankine, when asked by a parliamentary committee about the non-supply of tickets, replied: 'We do not use them . . . we have always found that many persons would not tell, or did not make up their minds, where they were going, which causes great confusion . . .'

One passenger recalled that travelling on the E & D meant 'you can examine the crops as you go along; you have time to hear the news from your companions'. Doubtless this conversation would be punctuated from time to time by bugle notes blown by the guard 'as the occasion requires'. The company even had the initiative to organize a bathers' special at six o'clock in the morning from St Leonard's to Portobello, advertised by exhorting the Edinburgh public 'to be up betimes, treating themselves to a pleasant ride and a refreshing bath, instead of the false luxury of a snooze in bed'.

Innocent or not, the Edinburgh & Dalkeith appears to have been highly successful in everything it attempted. Historian John Thomas pointed out that its passenger-carrying figures per mile of track were superior to those of its pioneering Stockton & Darlington and Liverpool & Manchester contemporaries. But it was really in coal transport that it excelled, playing a major part in the doubling of the amount of coal supplied to Edinburgh and Leith in the first half of the nineteenth century.

As early as 2 January 1844, the E & D Manager, David Rankine, was enquiring if a connection could be made between his system and the new-planned NBR. Negotiations between the two were opened shortly afterwards, although it might be more accurate to specify *three* companies, the Leith branch enjoying corporate autonomy from the rest of the Edinburgh & Dalkeith system. The Leith Railway suggested a junction between their line and the new railway at Portobello, with the former's gauge being widened to take NBR traffic. Matters were still not resolved when the North British company's Bill came to its committee stage at Westminster, where who should emerge as an objector to the NBR Bill but the E & D Railway Company (along with, amongst others, the Caledonian— whose representatives failed to put in an appearance).

With all but 242 out of 32,000 shares contracted for by 5 June, the North British was in a strong financial position, and not unreasonably decided to buy off the opposition in the most literal sense. This decision was, the shareholders were told, 'of very great importance to this company', and involved the purchase of the Edinburgh & Dalkeith main line, along with the Fisherrow branch (the more important Leith branch not being specified) for £113,000, but with the NBR being effectively indemnified against the smaller company's debts. On 22 June the new owners, the NBR stockholders, were told that the 'Innocent' line had just made an annual profit of £3,534, although the main reasons for purchase were to remove parliamentary opposition and to give access to the Midlothian coalfield '*and to Galashiels*'. A new Act of Parliament would be required to consolidate the purchase, payment to be made within three months of the Act becoming law. The E & D Company had to secure landowners' permission for locomotive operations, the engines being supplied by the NBR, who would be responsible for the cost of regauging. This last cost was to be some £33,000, almost half the cost of purchase, minus debts.

The new owners were soon asked to consider extending the existing E & D line inwards from St Leonard's to the chosen terminus at North Bridge by a new urban approach—this at a time when the NBR was already negotiating with landowners on what is now the main approach route through Edinburgh's eastern suburbs, one of these being disputed (with Miller of Craigentinny) right up to and into Parliament. There may have been some financial benefit to E & D shareholders if the St Leonard's approach had been adopted, but John Miller reported unfavourably—the NBR had already paid £100 for tunnelling rights through the Calton Hill—and St Leonard's was doomed to become a railway backwater, serving as a coal distribution centre for another 125 years.

The Leith branch was so important to the NBR that when problems arose in negotiating with the Leith Branch directors, and an offer by them to sell out to the NBR in September 1844 had to be refused, Miller was ordered to survey a possible branch from the new NBR line between Edinburgh and Portobello. The new company had already offered to pay for a connection at the latter point and half of the gauge-widening expenses, in return for full running powers for the NBR. There was an element of competition in all this as the Edinburgh, Leith & Newhaven (later Granton) Railway was already building a line from the city to its port, being slowed by engineering and estimating problems.

The North British could not afford to let this negotiating difficulty drag on too long; in retrospect, they might have been better to apply for permission to build their own branch to Leith, as they were considering, although possibly only to put pressure on the Leith Branch Directors. What later became the NBR's main approach to Leith Docks was a single-line (until around the First World War) connection from the Edinburgh-Berwick main line down to the former E & D from Portobello, and this was to take on the nature of a notorious bottleneck, ultimately making necessary the construction of the Lothian Lines (an extensive network of freight-only lines super-imposed on the existing NBR system in and around eastern Edinburgh at the time of the First World War). Indeed, even after the opening of the highly expensive Leith Central branch in 1903, the NBR still had no commodious entry into the docks except round by the Portobello incline. The only alternative—across Commercial Street level crossing, past North Leith station (actually the Leith terminus of the rival EL & G, taken over as the Edinburgh, Perth & Dundee in 1862)—was inconvenient and did not easily allow for on-site shunting.

Relations with the E & D took something of a downward turn in November 1844 with the Duke of Buccleuch, one of Scotland's largest landowners and a partner in the Lothians waggonway, disput-ing the cost of modernizing the E & D to main-line standards. The North British considered that His Grace was, as an E & D partner, required to honour the terms of the newly-signed agreement which would be presented to parliament as a Bill for the line's takeover; the matters in dispute appeared to include the cost of altering wagon axles, and the regauging costs of the Dalkeith branch. This latter line had been built by the Duke himself, and plainly there seems to have been a lack of consultation among the E & D directors on the matter. Although sure of their legal position, the NBR directors were not fool enough to antagonize such a powerful figure, the Board minutes indicating that a conference should be held with the Duke's agent, the NBR being prepared, the archives reveal, to concede where necessary 'as a matter of expediency', and this ultimately appears to have been what happened. Possession of the E & D came to the NBR on 1 October 1845, payment for the Leith Branch being completed the following December.

Meanwhile, work forged ahead on the construction of the first cross-Border line. One unexpected problem was the need to pay for the appointment of extra constables to restrain the behaviour of the navvies, a riot being reported at Cockburnspath in October 1845. Indeed, within three months the local minister there, the Reverend Paterson, was urging the Company to appoint a 'missionary' to tend to the obvious spiritual needs of the labourers, and £100 was laid aside for this purpose, although it is not clear from the records if an appointment was made. Six months later, following more disturbances, the Procurator Fiscal of Berwickshire was demanding £13 18s payment for the use of extra constables in the area, the NBR paying up immediately. Payment for batons, handcuffs and other appropriate equipment was also authorized, although the local County Council failed in a bid for NBR compensation for broken windows.

Nor was this the only problem encountered at Cockburnspath. When a Visiting Committee of Directors walked along the planned line of railway in the autumn of 1845, they were horrified by what they found on this section.

'There are several cuts and faces only one-half manned, and for about a mile, where heavy works have to be performed, not an individual is employed . . . (The workforce) looked as if they were emerging from a state of mutiny, sullen and discontented.'

Flooding had already exposed problems at the sites of the Pease and Tower Burns, while Penmanshiel tunnel (only some 267 yards) was only half dug, the remaining half estimated for a further nine months' work. The next contractor's section southwards, as far as Ayton, was a model of propriety in comparison, the directors being able to make part of their journey in waggons. Here, 'both men and horses are stouter and fatter and fresher', the contractor eschewing the use of a form of the 'truck' system known to the NBR directors as 'Tommy'.

This was an already infamous method of paying the labourers in tickets realizable for goods only in shops provided near the worksite by the contractor. The system was open to abuse—indeed, for that reason, it was already illegal in industry—as poor quality food and beer was often provided, the alternative being for the navvy to starve. According to the historian of the railway navvy, Terry Coleman, 'often contractors made more profit from truck than from the railway works themselves', and it does appear that Cockburnspath bank, the greatest incline from the outskirts of Edinburgh all the way to London (King's Cross) was the product of unfortunate workmen who had no alternative food sources to those supplied by a dishonest or, at best, uncaring contractor.

Ironically, as the opening date drew near in 1846, it was the Houndwood contract (ie the section immediately to the south of the Cockburnspath bank) which caused concern by being behind schedule. One hopes that this was not effectively a repudiation of the more enlightened employment practices of the contractors on this stretch, but certainly by June 1846, already well past the projected opening date of 1 May, the NBR was taking powers to complete the section, at the expense of the discredited contractor.

But, nearer to Berwick, problems of a different kind with another contractor reasserted themselves. The inspection party in 1845 were unhappy about the appearance of three bridges, while

'the embankments do not look well, and when it is considered that they are about 200 feet above the Sea, which is close underneath, the travelling public may be much alarmed.'

The Committee not surprisingly recommended the adoption of monthly reports from the construction sites comprising the line. The Directors may also have been contemplating one previously unforeseen result of accepting George Hudson's advice—the contractor whose work in the Berwickshire hills so displeased them was also a fairly important shareholder! Indeed, all the contractors, good and bad, conscientious or slapdash, had not inconsiderable influence within the company, thanks to the Board's policy of asking contractors to accept one-third of their payment in shares.

Earlier, the Plans Committee had visited the sites of the proposed stations, the most famous of these being 'The Castle of Berwick'. There is the smallest hint in the NBR archives that there was a contemporary awareness that a terrible deed was about to be done; in July 1844 a letter was received from the Misses Askew, presumably property owners in the town, regarding the preservation of the castle, but this was not mentioned again as the NBR proceeded to mortally demolish this ancient monument, and the company soon found it necessary to offer to take over more of the Askew land than originally intended, right down to the Tweed. In 1845 the NBR even prepared a parliamentary petition to protect their exclusive right to the station site, in case of possible encroachments on to the north bank of the Tweed by English companies.

One national edifice destined to be treated more respectfully by the railway juggernaut was the Palace and Abbey of Holyrood in Edinburgh. The North British line was to run about 200 yards to the east and north-east of the walls, and the Company's Directors were at their most sycophantic in ensuring no possible offence to the

Monarch. To support their Parliamentary Bill, the ecclesiastical architect William Burn was engaged to report on the possible nuisance to Holyrood (it must have been one of his last Edinburgh commissions; he apparently settled in London that year), and the Commissioners of Woods and Forests forced the NBR to agree to an extension of their Calton Hill tunnel, if required, and to hide the line in the palace's environs behind a wooden screen. Burn reported that there would be little environmental nuisance except possibly from noise; if decreed necessary by the Palace authorities, trains on this stretch would not be locomotive-powered during a royal sojourn at Holyrood. Luckily for the NBR, HM Queen Victoria turned out to be something of a railway enthusiast! One could only pity any horses having to pull trains up the 1 in 78 gradient into and through the Calton tunnel.

Permanent stations were decided upon in September 1845 for Portobello, Musselburgh (later Inveresk), Longniddry, Haddington, Linton, Dunbar, Cockburnspath, Ayton and Berwick, with temporary buildings at Joppa, Tranent or Prestonpans, Drem, Beltonford, Grantshouse and Reston 'until it was better ascertained from the traffic whether permanent stations should be erected at these places or elsewhere'. Berwick would have a 'Station keeper' salaried at £150 annually, plus a house, the Dunbar and Haddington 'keepers'

*What is left of Berwick Castle after it was demolished by the iconoclastic North British Railway can be seen in the foreground of this view of 'Deltic' No 55003* Meld *crossing the Royal Border Bridge with a northbound express in the late 1960s.* (D. Anderson)

receiving £100 plus housing. By the following summer, the list of payments did not include emoluments for staff at Joppa or Belton-ford, nor was there any mention of a station at Ballencrieff in East Lothian. George Dow pointed out in his centenary history that an 1846 NBR advertisement mentioned Gullane and Aberlady coaches running from Ballencrieff, but there is no mention of all this in the Board Minutes until November 1847, when it was decided to 'discontinue' stopping facilities there. In September 1846 there is a mention in the Minutes of a station at St Margaret's; its absence from the early station salary lists suggests that, if built, it may have been unstaffed; the inhabitants of Piershill had requested a station there even before the opening. Before the end of the year a contract was given out for the construction of a station at Innerwick, east of Dunbar.

Excitement began to mount in the office of the North British Railway in the first half of 1846 as Scotland's first line to England inched towards reality. Staff appointments were made—the company's secretary Charles Davidson became General Manager at £1,000 pa, with James Bell as Line Superintendent and Robert Thornton in charge of the locomotive stock. The delivery of the engines, ordered in August 1844, is not noted in the company's Minutes, although there is evidence that some of them were being leased by the Edinburgh & Glasgow in the spring, and in February Hawthorn's were specifically asked to deliver one to the Berwick end of the line, presumably by sea.

The first steam locomotives designed to cross the border were (apart from contractors' engines) 38 Hawthorn-built 0-4-2s, 0-6-0s and 2-2-2s. Six of each of the latter two types were ordered in October 1845 for service on the Edinburgh & Dalkeith line, but as this was not ready for locomotive operations even a year later, they would undoubtedly have been used on the Berwick line to begin with. Full technical details of these machines are given in George Dow's work.

Two million tickets were ordered from McDonald and McIver, Glasgow, in preparation for the opening, costed at 2/5d (12p) and 1/10d (9p) per thousand, depending on size. In January 1846 the NBR enquired of pioneering ticket designer Thomas Edmondson 'the terms on which he would allow this company to use his patent apparatus', and the tickets appear to have been the standard Edmondson design from the first. Passenger rates per mile were decided at 2d, 1½d and 1d for first, second and third class. Co-ordinating arrangements were made with coaching firms already operating between Berwick and Newcastle, the fare being fixed at 21s (£1.05) inside and 13s (65p) outside the coach respectively between those towns. As a result of this road-rail co-operation, the earliest tickets specified 'First Class & Inside' for those lucky enough to be able to afford guaranteed protection against the elements for the whole journey between Edinburgh and Newcastle.

To keep track of the hours, an order was placed with a local firm of clockmakers but the Company also experimented by approving the purchase of an electric clock. An electric telegraph was authorized by the Board immediately after opening, although its cost later appeared to confine its length to between Edinburgh station (as the Board Minutes call it) and St Margaret's. A rule book 'to be observed by the engine-men, firemen, guards, porters, gatemen, pointsmen, platemen and others working on the line' was sent to the Board of Trade in April 1846 and formally approved by the company's own Board on 11 May.

Despite these preparations, when it must have seemed that the Border was indeed about to be crossed by trains for the first time, the NBR Directors realized that the Grantshouse-Ayton section was simply not ready, and the Board of Trade had to be informed accordingly. The official inspection was to take place on 5 May—in itself delayed from the earlier plan of a 1 May opening date—but it was 15 May before General Pasley finally inspected the line. Even this date, it proved, was too soon—the new railway was still not ready.

It was at this time that the Company itself took on responsibility for finishing the Houndwood (south of Grantshouse) contract, but immediately had to contend with an embankment slippage at Burnmouth. Equally bad was a case of sabotage at Monktonhall, where a rail was deliberately removed shortly before a works train arrived. Fortunately, there was no loss of life in either incident (a £20 reward was offered for the apprehension of the saboteur), but the North British certainly did not have its troubles to seek. Not surprisingly, the Board of Trade appears to have refused a request for an interim opening between Edinburgh and Cockburnspath, but demanded a second inspection, scheduled for 16 June. Ironically, the NBR had meanwhile refused to lend more of its engines to the Edinburgh & Glasgow on the over-optimistic grounds that it had urgent need of them itself.

Fortunately, this was proved to be true after the second Board of Trade inspection, for on Thursday 18 June 1846, the first passenger trains crossed the Anglo-Scottish border at Lamberton. This was not the opening to ordinary traffic—that took place the following Monday 22nd—but a ceremonial working of two enormous trains between Edinburgh and Berwick and back again. It was a day of celebration, of toasts and speechifying, and it was to end in a tragedy, one not mentioned in the histories of the company.

Watched by hundreds of spectators at the new but still incomplete North Bridge station in Edinburgh, many of them on the slopes of the nearby Calton Hill, trains were ceremonially flagged off to the Border, *to England*, at 10.05 and 10.37. The first of these comprised 12 coaches, mostly first class (to which were attached a further 12 at Dunbar), with four locomotives providing the motive power. The second train comprised no fewer than 26 coaches, with 'five engines yoked to it', as the *Scotsman*'s correspondent put it. Not surprisingly,

*Vanished from the East Coast Main Line in Scotland just as effectively as its steam predecessors, Class '46' No D175 is seen powering an up King's Cross relief train past the down Border sign on 8 August 1969. (Ian S. Carr)*

this mechanical caravan failed to climb Cockburnspath at the first attempt, being brought to a stop at Penmanshiel tunnel mouth 'to replenish the boilers'. The delay was apparently lengthened by the water being added cold, 'and of course time was consumed in bringing it to boiling pitch'.

In passing Lamberton, the newspaper made the valid point that the new North British Railway was not only the first to cross the Border but was doing so by the lowest pass through the southern uplands between the Irish Channel and the German Ocean, as the North Sea was called in those days. Commenting that Cockburnspath pass was 369 feet above sea level—the same height, it helpfully informed its readers, as the drawbridge at Edinburgh Castle—it compared this to 600 feet at Cumnock (on what later became the GSWR line), 1,000 feet at Beattock, and about 900 feet around the source of the Gala Water (ie Falahill). All three of these passes were eventually to bear Anglo-Scottish railways, all posing longer or stiffer gradients that the one which had brought the NBR's chain of five locomotives to a temporary halt.

The *Scotsman* waxed lyrical about the landscape encountered on this first journey southwards ('magnificent scenery, which in our opinion, can scarely be matched except in the most sequestered glens in the Highlands'), and said of the train itself:

'To bystanders the sight must have been extremely imposing, especially at the curvatures, where the monster train was seen to bend to the right and left, and display a flexibility of a silken cord, while rivalling the eagle's flight in speed.'

At Berwick the trippers were able to examine the Elizabethan

*Although some miles north of the Border crossing at Lamberton, this mid-1950s shot of 'A3' No 60090* Grand Parade *was too good to exclude, showing a 'Pacific' working hard on Cockburnspath bank on an up express, just south of the now closed Penmanshiel tunnel. Unusually for a Haymarket engine, the buffer-beam could do with more than a lick of paint.* (John Robertson)

fortifications, along with what the North British Railway had left of the castle, before entraining once more. A lengthy stop was then made at Dunbar where a ceremonial dinner was served. A sumptuous repast for 700 guests was the order of the day, the wines alone costing the Company almost £150, and these were employed in a programme of toasts to handsel in the new railway. Deputy Chairman Eagle Henderson led the speeches, which were only concluded with the trains departing for Edinburgh at 5 and 6 o'clock respectively.

The newspaper reaction to the appearance and operation of the new railway was generally favourable, indeed almost enthusiastic, although the main Edinburgh paper did say:

'We must give the Directors a hint about their third-class carriages. They will never do in summer . . . We travelled from Dunbar to Edinburgh and never in our life experienced such a stew . . .'

Significantly, the Board took heed—at their meeting on 24 June, the Directors ordered the vehicles to be altered to improve ventilation.

But the day did not end entirely in celebration. The *Scotsman* reported that railwayman Matthew Howat, adjusting oil lighting on the roof of a coach when in motion, was struck by a passing bridge in the Longniddry area and later died in the city's Royal Infirmary of a fractured skull. 'He was quite sober when the accident happened,' opined the paper. There is no record of the incident in the NBR's Board Minutes, and no indication of compensation being paid.

Financial problems were to lead to a complete review of the NBR's operations within two years, and from this later report we learn that the first line across the Border was laid with 70 lb rail in 16 feet lengths on 3,535 sleepers per mile. The earliest locomotives averaged 110 miles daily.

'The promoters have determined to avoid all useless expense in ornamental works at stations and otherwise . . . *not a sixpence* shall be expended unnecessarily!' Within fifty years, railway author William Acworth was to wryly observe that no one could accuse the North British Railway of failing in its promise to be as parsimonious as possible in its station decorations. He was referring to the state of Edinburgh's two main NBR stations—Waverley and Haymarket— shortly before the opening of the Forth Bridge. Ironic that the wording of a shareholders' prospectus of 1843, before a yard of track was laid, should come home to haunt the North British Railway.

*     *     *

Six weeks after the opening of the line to Berwick by the North British, its western neighbour, the Edinburgh & Glasgow, completed its controversial transit of Princes Street Gardens, including tunnels through the Mound and the city's West End, from Haymarket, the former eastern terminus of the line from Glasgow (Queen St). On 14 January 1846 the NBR had formally approved traffic-sharing with the E & G as well as the Scottish Central Railway, with whom it had no physical connection at that time. Such a close working relationship with the E & G should come as no suprise, given their sharing of a chairman, John Learmonth, but was surely to start a rail tradition which was to result in the two companies merging in 1865, effectively giving the NBR the key to central Scotland and its largest city. This was despite the E & G's close working relationship with the Caledonian in the 1850s.

Interestingly, Learmonth had achieved the chairmanship of the E & G largely due to the pressure from the Sabbatarian lobby on the previous incumbent, and the NBR soon learned how powerful this could be. Apart from a formal motion at every half-yearly NBR shareholders' meeting by a Mr Blackadder to prevent Sunday workings, the Company's first taste of this came when it ran foul of a powerful opponent after barely a fortnight's operation.

Early in July, possibly after only one Sunday's working—there were Sunday trains southwards from Edinburgh at 08.00 and 19.30, with trains from Berwick at 06.42 and 17.22—a NBR driver called Thomas Weddell found himself summonsed by Sir Andrew Agnew for operating a locomotive on the Sabbath. Agnew was nationally famous for his support of Lord's Day Observance and only nine years previously had succeeded in steering a parliamentary bill through its second reading which would have prohibited any work on a Sunday unless it was adjudged an act of necessity or mercy. In 1837, however, William IV's death caused a parliamentary dissolution which prevented the bill's further progress. But this was of little compensation to poor Weddell; at least his employers decided to defend the case, but its progress does not appear to be recorded in the Minutes. Nor was this the only evidence of Sunday chauvinism, the directors having to give an audience to a protesting delegation from the Free Church of Scotland, as well as letters from the Presbytery of Edinburgh and Free Church communities along the East Lothian coast. It was a force which the North British would ignore at its peril.

A more immediate problem for the new railway was an accident in July when an engine and three coaches were derailed on the Markle embankment. The line's locomotive superintendent, Robert Thornton, was accompanying the train (the 04.30 out of Edinburgh) and was injured, along with the driver. No passengers were hurt in an incident blamed entirely by the NBR on recently heavy rains.

It must have been a bad summer for precipitation; on 30 September the Minutes record that 'Due to heavy rain since Monday last, certain of the bridges on the line had fallen or were otherwise injured'. The line was effectively severed and questions were asked about the quality of the earlier workmanship. The Board of Trade was called in, General Pasley making another inspection on 27 October, when bridges in the Beltonford area (immediately west of Dunbar) appear to have been the centre of the problem. Most unusually, the police expressed concern about the state of a bridge at Portobello—there was a viaduct with one iron and 11 wooden arches here, spanning the Leith Branch of the newly acquired Edinburgh & Dalkeith—but the NBR referred this enquirer to the Board of Trade. George Dow believed that the railway had been opened before the line had been properly allowed to consolidate, and he recorded that it was well into 1847 before public misgivings on the matter had been allayed.

Meanwhile, the new railway had to fight another battle. The autumn of 1846 saw considerable manoeuvrings amongst railway stockholders to secure an amalgamation between the York, Newcastle & Berwick and North British Railways. That this was done by somewhat underhand means, with a newspaper advertisement placed without the Board's approval, is suggested by a letter sent by NBR chairman John Learmonth to the 'Railway King' George Hudson himself on 14 November suggesting that if the latter wished to discuss amalgamation:

'you should have the kindness to do so direct with me . . . we have had some works on the line severely injured, but with one exception all have been substantially restored already. The damages have been grossly exaggerated in the newspaper, but all (companies?) have their enemies, and we cannot expect to escape. I have no knowledge whatever of the anonymous notice for a Bill for the amalgamation of our company with yours and do not know whether to contradict it or not . . .'

Within two years, the NBR Directors were forced to approach Hudson with a similar proposal of their own. As related in the chapter on the Waverley Route, the construction of the northern part of that line, as far as Hawick, coincided with a new trade recession which dissuaded many shareholders from answering the company's calls for capital in 1848. On 23 September a party of directors was led by Learmonth to Berwick where a conference was planned to take place with Hudson, but this was cancelled and rearranged for Newcastle for 14 October. This proved to be another wasted journey, the York, Newcastle & Berwick Company declining to either buy or lease the North British, which was valued at £4.1 million. Historian John Thomas believes that the North British Directors were prepared to sell out to their southern neighbour at this time, the English company failing to confirm what the Edinburgh directors took to be an informal bid.

Adding to the NBR's problems as the halfway point of the century neared was a fightback by shipping companies on Britain's east coast, whose reduced rates undoubtedly affected rail traffic. Expectations of cross-Border traffic had been high; it had been estimated that some 25,000 passengers travelled between the English and Scottish capitals by ship before the Railway Age, and prospective shareholders had been told that the coming of the railway would increase this number. In fact to begin with, rail-borne passengers tallied only 5,700 with twice as many still voyaging by sea. As late as 1855 there were as many shipping companies offering berths to London from Edinburgh as

*Resplendent in its two-tone green livery, Class '47' D1766 passes the up Border sign on the 10.05 Edinburgh-King's Cross on 8 August 1969.* (Ian S. Carr)

there had been ten years previously. In 1849, the SS *Britannia* conveyed passengers between Newcastle and Leith in 10 hours at 10s (50p) return cabin class or 6s second class. Possibly in some spirit of retribution, the NBR directors resolved in March 1849 to withdraw free passes for shipwrecked sailors!

*    *    *

As railway enthusiasts know, it was to be nearly another 80 years before there would be a corporate union between the North British Company and its working allies to the south of the Tweed. On 1 January 1923, as Britain's railways attempted to pick themselves up from the unprecedented demands of the First World War, with its grossly swollen traffic demands having to be dealt with at a time of staff diminution and rising costs, amalgamation may have seemed the only solution.

The North British section between Edinburgh and Berwick was unique in Anglo-Scottish railway operations—indeed, unique throughout Britain's main-line railways—in allowing the operation of its most important traffic by another company, even into its operational centre, Edinburgh. In 1862 the NBR and North Eastern Railway (successor to the YN & B) concluded an agreement, not effective until 1869, by which the latter company attained running powers over the 58 miles from Berwick into Edinburgh in return for the Scottish company being given reciprocal powers for its Border Counties trains between Hexham and Newcastle.

It was, on the face of it, an astonishing agreement for the NBR to concede, nor does understanding it become any easier after mature reflection. Although only 4 miles longer than the East Coast line, there was no question of the Border Counties Railway, as discussed later in this book, rivalling the line through Berwick as an Anglo-Scottish trunk route. Historians appear mixed in their attitude to this agreement; E. L. Ahrons declared that the North British had 'sold their birthright for a mess of pottage', although one of the company's own historians, the late John Thomas, argued that the arrangement worked in everyone's favour, not least that of the travelling public. In fact, a passenger's reasonable expectation of travelling non-stop, or at least uninterrupted, between Edinburgh and Newcastle, could have been met equally well by the NBR and NER sharing through workings, with a possible numerical superiority of services in favour of the English company, who owned a higher mileage between the two cities.

Successive NBR Boards would not appear to have held a similar view to Thomas's in their interpretation of the 1862 treaty, contesting their own agreement in no fewer than 11 tribunals and two visits to the House of Lords. In 1897 the Edinburgh company went as far as wresting from the NER the operation of express trains north of Berwick, something which the York-based company did not immediately oppose. They were doubtless aware that the NBR's act of

*High above the Tweed, 'A4' 'Pacific' No 60024 Kingfisher comes off the Royal Border Bridge and slows for the Berwick stop, with a King's Cross-Glasgow express on 29 August 1960.* (Ian S. Carr)

defiance could not be sustained indefinitely; for one thing, the North British had no crossover at the south end of Berwick station, this facility being situated on the northern end of the Royal Border Bridge in NER territory. With North British engines being denied access to this crossover, southbound trains had to be reversed out of the station for their engines to be removed at great expense of time, something the North Eastern might not work too hard to make up southbound before handing over to the Great Northern, thus ensuring that the southern partner was aware of the cause of the unpunctuality.

Not only that, but one of the subsidiary clauses of the 1862 agreement allowed the NBR something of a free hand in taking over a neighbouring company without North Eastern interference in return for NER running powers over the North British system to Glasgow and Perth. These had never been enforced, but in 1897 the Edinburgh Company was simply digging itself into an even deeper pit by its efforts to run its own traffic to Berwick in defiance of the agreement. To add insult to injury, the expresses appeared to need double-heading on the NBR section!

This act of defiance by the NBR did not last, particularly with the NER making enquiries about sending its own trains through to Glasgow. By 1904 a new agreement appeared to regularize the source of this pathetic conflict, very much in favour of the English Company.

By that time the rails at Lamberton had carried no fewer than three sets of racing trains in 1888, 1895 and 1901, in separate passages of long-distance competitive communication without parallel in British railway annals.

In 1888 the object was to finish first at Edinburgh with the 10.00 daytime departures from King's Cross and Euston. The western partners were the London & North Western and Caledonian companies, the former handing over the 'baton' to the latter at Carlisle. Seven years later an even more competitive episode of racing began, with Aberdeen the target for the respective East and West Coast 20.00 night departures from London. In both years, the North Eastern ran the Berwick-Edinburgh stretch—and with some distinction—the North British only entering the fray in 1895 when operating north of Edinburgh across the Forth and Tay bridges.

The story of these races is too complex to tell here, the reader being referred to O. S. Nock's excellent book *The Railway Race to the North*. As for the third race, in 1901, this was unlike the previous two outbursts of competitive operation in having a *third* participant in a contest to reach Edinburgh first by three different lines, including the Midland/North British route from St Pancras to Edinburgh via Leicester and the Settle and Carlisle and Waverley Routes. The result was to produce the finest times ever recorded over the last-named line, as related in the relevant chapter in this book. In 1901 the North Eastern simply repeated the good work it had performed in 1888 and 1895, except for the obstacle of being purposely held up by NBR signalmen at, and north of, Berwick, who were understandably giving their own train, over to the west among the Border hills, a better chance!

It must be said that this 1901 race was very much the product of the poor relationship between the North British and North Eastern railways, with the latter, along with its Great Northern partner farther south, constantly suspecting that the NBR would throw in its lot with the Midland. Yet the Midland was equally suspicious of the NBR's historic links with its working partner at Berwick—so much so that on one occasion the Midland complained that the North British was displaying too many East Coast posters at Waverley! Yet on 1 November 1900, for example, relations between the NBR and NER were so bad that the former's signalman quite intentionally held up the down 'Flying Scotsman' at Berwick as the North Eastern was running it to a schedule which the Edinburgh company had not agreed to.

Headed by 'S' Class 4-6-0 No 2010, the 275-ton express arrived at the Border town 1½ minutes early, having run from Newcastle in the very creditable time of 69½ minutes. However, this put it well ahead of its booked time (as far as the North British was concerned), so its signalman refused to give it the road. 'For 18½ minutes the NB officials held up the train,' thundered no less an organ than *The Times*, 'while the officials enjoyed a chat on the squalid platforms, and the passengers fumed and made indignant remarks.' Finally released, like a greyhound from a trap, No 2010 tore up the line to Edinburgh, before experiencing an irritating series of signal delays, its arrival time at Waverley being 1 minute late by the unofficial NER timetable and 14 minutes early by the public NBR one.

In other words, battles between the English and Scots did not entirely die out in the Berwick area with the Union of the Crowns! In retrospect it seems tragic that the two companies which met there could not have engineered a better working relationship—in particular, it might have led to a more sensible timetable on the Tweed Valley line, as discussed later. It would seem unarguable that both companies were basically unjustified in suspecting each other's conduct and motives. If the North British appeared to be prepared to reach Newcastle at all costs—even over the Border Counties line if all else failed—that was probably only true of the Board in 1862. Later NBR attempts to renegotiate that agreement might well have been dealt with more sympathetically; certainly the NER only exacerbated the conflict by coming to an agreement with, of all people, the Caledonian in 1898 to send two through coaches per day between Newcastle and Glasgow via Carlisle. (The NER's predecessor, the York, Newcastle and Berwick, had suggested such a routeing of Anglo-Scottish traffic as early as October 1847, presumably with Newcastle & Carlisle Railway approval; the Caledonian had then rejected the idea out of hand for fear of offending the Edinburgh & Glasgow whose line it was hoping to lease when financial conditions improved).

*Berwick-on-Tweed station on 30 April 1964 with the twin towers of the goods hoist (now dismantled) prominent. BR '4MT' No 76050 has just travelled tender-first along the Tweed Valley line with the 16.02 from St Boswells, having reversed at Tweedmouth. (Douglas Hume)*

The NBR's relationship with the Midland—which provided its East Coast partners with apparent grounds for suspicion of the Edinburgh Company's goodwill—was hardly a rewarding one in the long term for either Derby or Edinburgh. Indeed, Waverley Route services at one time had to be subsidized by the Midland, who must have wondered if their massive investment in the Forth Bridge had been worthwhile.

After 1923, the whole question of uneasy relationships between English and Scottish companies became nothing more than one of academic history. The creation of the LNER swept the NBR and NER into the same grouping, although the new administrators were quick to recognize Berwick as an organizational boundary between the North Eastern and Scottish areas. As discussed in the chapter on the Tweed Valley line, the NBR roundhouse shed was closed in 1924 and the station at last rebuilt by 1927. Unlike the previous arrangement of up and down platforms, connected by a narrow footbridge, and with nothing more than a waiting room on the down side, the LNER gave the Border town an 800-foot island platform with a glazed roof for 240 feet and with ancillary services across the footbridge at the public entrance on the up side. The previous 5 mph speed restriction was greatly improved, particularly for down traffic.

The Border signs (14 feet across at their widest extent and 9 feet high) were erected at Lamberton in the first half of 1937. They have been there ever since, although they have been removed for repainting when necessary. In particular, passengers arriving at platforms 20 and 21 at Edinburgh Waverley in 1958 must have been astonished to find the England-Scotland sign decorating the platform!

*LNER 'Hush-hush' No 10000 heads a short East Coast express, perhaps an Edinburgh-Newcastle relief, past Tweedmouth on an unknown afternoon sometime between 1931 and 1935. Berwick-on-Tweed can be seen on the other side of the river in this previously unpublished picture, which has only just been rediscovered in a commercial photographer's archives.*
(courtesy R. Clapperton)

# CARHAM

## Tweed Valley line

Today the site of Carham station is not even shown on the 1:50,000 Ordnance Survey map, while of the Border crossing itself, only a couple of hundred yards away, no rail evidence remains.

Carham station, closed on 4 July 1955, was an unusual configuration of staggered up and down platforms—not uncommon in the former North Eastern Railway area but unusual in Scotland where Gorebridge and Heriot on the Waverley Route were other rare examples. The actual 'frontier' east of Carham is marked by a stream or burn which empties into the Tweed not far to the north. The station, incidentally, is in Scotland, the village it served being in England as the Border itself continues on its diagonal path across the landscape.

The second-last stop on the North Eastern Railway's Tweedmouth-Kelso branch before Kelso was reached, Carham was perhaps less interesting than its western neighbour, Sprouston. As well as a double platform, this last stop before Kelso boasted a one-road engine shed, from which the NER operated its Kelso-Tweedmouth services, Kelso station being the territory of the North British Railway, with whom the NER had a continually uneasy relationship. The shed's list of occupants included a very distinguished Second World War 'evacuee'—none other than the GWR 4-4-0 *City of Truro*, sent there from the then York Railway Museum. According to North Eastern Railway historian Ken Hoole, the shed appears to have been rebuilt in 1882 after its predecessor had been blown down in a gale. It closed as a working depot in 1916 as an economy measure.

Carham and Sprouston share an unusual railway distinction with Annan (Shawhill), of being the only stations built in Scotland by an English pre-Grouping railway company. On 27 July 1849 the York, Newcastle & Berwick Railway, which merged into the North Eastern in 1854, began operations along the Tweed valley as far as Sprouston

*So changed is the site of Carham station nowadays that the author was at first unable to recognize it from this 1962 photograph. The NER-style buildings – all but unique in Scotland – are now demolished but the staggered up and down platforms remain on either side of the level crossing site. The platform to the left in this photograph is the loading-bay, while out of sight to the right is the Tweed flowing eastwards to Tweedmouth, also the destination for tender-first '2MT' 2-6-0 No 46473 with its pick-up freight. The locomotive will cross the Border about two hundred yards east of here. (Douglas Hume)*

from Tweedmouth (the latter town is a satellite of Berwick-on-Tweed on the other side of the river, as Gateshead is to Newcastle).

The North British did not reach Kelso until the following summer when it opened a temporary station just west of the town; an end-on junction was not properly established until the summer of 1851. The actual boundary was considered to be 1 mile west of Sprouston, 1¾ miles from Kelso, the only reasonably large-sized town in the area. After Grouping in 1923, the former companies' boundaries on the line remained intact, but after Nationalization in 1948 the Scottish Region's territory expanded eastwards as far as the 'frontier' at Carham, and appropriate Border signs were erected in about 1950. But even after this time, old company prejudices remained; ScR working timetables showed nothing east of Carham except departure or arrival times at Tweedmouth.

\*    \*    \*

The valley—so broad it is more of a plain—first had a railway mooted for it as early as 1806. Although conceived as more of a waggonway than a railway, the Berwick & Kelso line would have transported barley and other agricultural products to the sea at Spittal (Tweedmouth), in turn importing coal and lime from the coast. After an enthusiastic initial meeting was held at Kelso in 1806, a survey was authorized, and its resulting report was issued by John Rennie in November 1809 (one historian gives 1811 as the report's date), and this produced some interesting data.

The waggonway would have comprised 22 miles of single track, but with works constructed to allow for possible doubling. The cost would have been £90,000 at £4,091 per mile. One local landowner suggested keeping down the costs by donating land to the railway concern, something which certainly did not happen on the western side of Kelso, as related later. Some 31,000 tons of coal and lime were anticipated annually as westbound cargo, with up to 10,000 tons of agricultural product going to the coast. One potential snag was the bridging of the Tweed, Rennie's estimate allowing for contributions from local authorities; Kelso is on the north side of the river, bridged by Rennie himself for road traffic in 1803, while Tweedmouth's harbour facilities are on the south side. Some Berwick merchants insisted that the line be brought into their town, on the north side of the river, and there does seem to have been some controversy about its planned route. Its probable course would have been roughly over that of the succeeding Tweed Valley line, the difference being that the latter did not cross the Tweed.

Incorporated on 31 May 1811, it is believed to be the first railway project whose Act of Incorporation specified carrying passengers. (In the event, the Kilmarnock & Troon Railway seems to have become the first Scottish railway to actually transport passengers.) Despite local interest, renewed from time to time, the idea came to nothing, being formally abandoned in 1838.

Other railway projects were proposed for the area. Kelso to Berwick would have been just one part of a grandiose scheme to link Glasgow with the mouth of the Tweed by waggonway. A plan produced by Thomas Telford in 1807 postulated 125 miles of double track built at around £3,000 per mile. Two 'inclined plains' were included in the plans, both west of the Tweed Valley.

*No passenger had glimpsed this Anglo-Scottish border crossing sign at Carham, on the Tweed Valley line, for nearly three years when this picture was taken in April 1967. By this time the line was closed west of Kelso, while the former NER section from there to Tweedmouth was singled and used only by the occasional freight. (R. B. McCartney)*

Other abortive schemes included the Roxburgh & Selkirk tramway and the Kelso, Melrose & Dalkeith Railway of 1817. The former, supported by Sir Walter Scott amongst others, was to be financed by government grant, its promoters insisting that this would ultimately allow mineral traffic to travel 'toll-free'. The latter's route was surveyed in 1820 by Glasgow's Robert Stevenson but would have lacked outlets to north or south. Although not implemented, one historian reports that capital of £55,000 was raised for the latter scheme within a month.

In 1845, with the Railway Mania at its height, the Caledonian Extension was proposed, comprising a cross-country line from Ayr, bisecting the Caledonian's main line to the south near Carstairs and then on through Peebles, Galashiels and Kelso to Berwick. This succeeded in challenging both the Ayrshire interests on the west coast and the NBR on both of its lines south and south-eastward from Edinburgh. Additionally, there was the potential threat of traffic from the Newcastle direction taking to Caledonian metals for Glasgow or even, rather circuitously, for Edinburgh. This was a recurring spectre which haunted North British thinking; indeed, before the end of the century both the North Eastern and Caledonian Railways were programming through coach movements between their systems at Carlisle, in order to teach the NBR a lesson during a period of unease between the Edinburgh and York Companies.

The North British was much exercised in 1845 by this threat from the Caledonian's Extension scheme. Commenting that the latter concern 'had no local connection with or interest in the District', the NBR's shareholders were given evidence of the unfavourable distances envisaged should Parliament be so unwise as to allow the interloper into the Tweed basin—Kelso to Carlisle by Hawick at 66½ miles, compared to Kelso to Carlisle by Caledonian at 124½ miles. As emphasized in the chapter on the Waverley Route, the North British was making no claims for that line as a possible future outlet to the south, the vague term 'West of England' being the most they were prepared to claim as a target destination. Obviously there was no point in alienating George Hudson when all the rails between Edinburgh and Berwick were still not laid.

The Extension scheme collapsed with so many other Mania projects, and in February 1846 the NBR and Caledonian agreed to make Peebles the dividing line between their systems (although not a yard of track existed there).

Practical measures to bring a railway to the Tweed basin began in the spring of 1845 when the North British ordered a survey of a branch serving the area, the shareholders being told that this would be 10 miles long, running from near St Boswells via Roxburgh, where the Teviot would be bridged. At Kelso it was proposed to unite with a line from the Berwick direction, built by whichever of the rival English enterprises triumphed in the current rivalry in Parliament to drive northwards from Newcastle. A Jedburgh branch was also envisaged, its Town Council being particularly enthusiastic.

Progress on the building of the Tweed Valley line by the Scottish company slowed almost to a stop as the 1840s drew to a close. After Parliamentary approval for the branch had been obtained in 1846, work was suspended in September 1849 when the NBR began to realize that its branches, particularly the Hawick line, were less likely to add revenue to the network as to drain it of vitality. St Boswells served as the terminus of the line from Edinburgh from June 1849 until opening through to Hawick in November. However, the Kelso branch's major feature, the Teviot bridge, was not apparently begun until March of that year (there was a report of an accident there in June), but there was a problem about the approach to Kelso, where the all-powerful Duke of Roxburgh apparently forbade a station in the town itself, on the north bank of the Tweed.

In contrast, the York, Newcastle & Berwick was forging ahead with its branch from the east. Indeed, during the NBR/YN & B amalgamation talks in 1848, the *Newcastle Journal* speculated that the Tweed Valley line would be an admirable jumping-off point for the construction of a line to Edinburgh independent of the then crisis-ridden North British. In turn, a Scottish investors' periodical saw this suggestion as a means of depressing NBR share values at a time when Hudson was looking to take over the Edinburgh Company. In other words, like Peebles, Kelso was a pleasant Border town being eyed by more than one company for its strategic significance.

One indication of how the Kelso branch was more than a minor expense for the North British was a land sale, referred to in Elliot's thesis (see Bibliography), whereby Sir George Douglas was congratulated by another landowner for having negotiated 'one of the most favourable Railway Transactions ever made in Scotland'. This probably refers to a NBR decision on 22 July 1846 to pay him £25,000, without discussion in the Board meeting. No wonder the Kelso line took so long to build!

While the North British succeeded in reaching Kelso in July 1850, it was nearly a year behind the York, Newcastle & Berwick in bringing rails to the Tweed Valley, the line from Tweedmouth opening to Sprouston on 27 July 1849. An impressive two-platform station was erected there, very conveniently for the village, and, as we have noted, a one-road engine-shed. This latter continued in use even after the NBR had built a larger depot at Kelso, complete with turntable. But there was still no connection between the two lines.

This did not materialize until June 1851, when an end-on junction was forged at Mellendean Burn, less than 2 miles west of Sprouston, one sharp-eyed railway enthusiast claiming that the junction was still detectable in later years because of the different ballast used by the two companies!

In November 1854 the North British decided to charge its English neighbour £370 annually for the use of Kelso station. It also, intriguingly, appeared to be considering suggesting four through

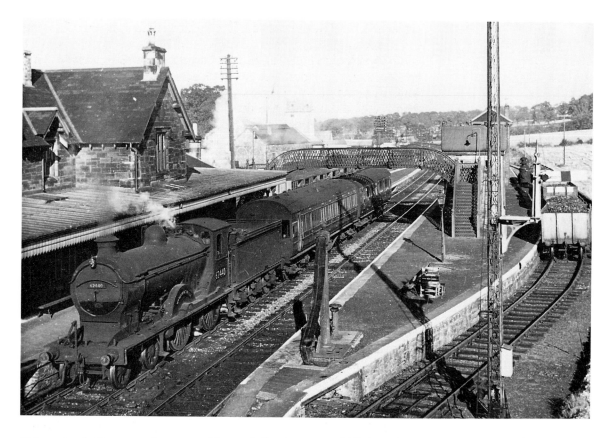

*Kelso station, looking east, with the delightfully-named former North British 'D30' 4-4-0 No 62440 Wandering Willie waiting to leave on a local for St Boswells. This 1950s shot shows the rural location of the station, well outside Kelso, which was on the other bank of the Tweed to the north. (A. A. Maclean)*

workings daily between Edinburgh and Berwick via the Tweed Valley, with the North Eastern being invited to operate one of them, presumably as far as St Boswells. If only this sensible scheme of operation had been adopted from such an early date, the line's passenger operation might have been more remunerative and longer-lasting. Indeed, on looking through the record of perverse train scheduling in the Tweed Valley, one is tempted to wonder why the companies bothered to join up at Mellendean at all. Certainly, such a junction created a new through route, but this was only used in emergencies, never more profitably than in 1948.

The Tweed Valley line's potential as an emergency diversion was so well demonstrated for three months in 1948 that the episode is worth examining in some detail. In August of that year, the railways throughout the Scottish Borders were blitzed by a rainstorm of unprecedented magnitude, and largely unexplained origin. Some 400 million tons of water deluged the Southern Uplands in a 24-hour period, with the storm centre near the town of Berwick, but with its effects being felt as far north as Edinburgh.

To make matters worse, rainfall had already been heavy in the previous week, and many rivers were in spate *before* the rains came in earnest on Thursday 12 August. So great was the precipitation that the Tweed broke its previous flood level at Kelso—by 3½ feet!

Needless to say, the railways were overwhelmed. Surface flooding was a problem in station locations, but more serious was the softening of earthworks, with embankments and cuttings taking on the consistency of melting chocolate. The Tweed line was soon blocked at the frontier-point of Carham, although this was a minor problem, and soon rectified, compared to the disasters which befell the two main ex-NBR routes to Edinburgh.

The East Coast line was blocked in no fewer than 13 places north of Berwick, with six bridges being entirely swept away between Grantshouse and Reston and six landslides occurring in other locations. An embankment near Ayton became a dam for floodwater which built up to the extent that a new lake 5 miles long, 300 yards wide and up to 40 feet deep threatened to overwhelm the coastal town of Eyemouth, which had already had its branch railway breached by a collapsing viaduct pier. Coastguards had to stand a 24-hour guard to fire warning rockets over the town if the new 'dam' broke. Mercifully, it held.

Three freights were trapped on this Berwick-Dunbar section, and it was some days before their loads could be transferred to road. A passenger train was stuck overnight at Chirnside on the Reston-St Boswells line, while even expresses on the main line were not immune. Three daytime expresses from King's Cross, the 09.50, 10.00 (non-stop 'Flying Scotsman') and 10.05 trains all had to be diverted; the first via Tweedmouth and the Tweed Valley before the Carham landslip, the others having to reverse down the ECML to Newcastle and then travel north via Carlisle and the Waverley Route, the 10.05 leading.

Not that the Waverley Route had escaped the meteorological holocaust. Conditions were not quite as bad as farther east, and the

*Blue-liveried 'A4' N0 60031* Golden Plover *takes water at Tweedmouth on a London-bound express during the 1948 floods emergency when East Coast traffic was rerouted by the Tweed Valley line.* (W. E. Boyd collection)

09.50 managed to battle through before the line became impassible, reaching Edinburgh 200 minutes late. Landslides soon blocked the line at Gorebridge, Tynehead, Heriot and Stow, with Galashiels station flooded. The 10.05 steamed into the worsening conditions north of Galashiels and had no sooner laboured over Falahill summit when it became immovably stranded at Tynehead. Class 'A2' No 60519 *Honeyway* could go no farther; when her driver telephoned to inform Control of the conditions, he was standing up to his waist in water. The unfortunate passengers had to wait for rescue by a convoy of seven chartered buses from Edinburgh the next morning. One less than grateful passenger was a goat travelling in the guard's van; its feeding having been forgotten in the excitement, it extracted revenge by eating much of the upholstery of the replacement bus!

The down 'Flying Scotsman' was stopped at Hawick when the above intelligence became known, and another reversal of direction, all the way back to Carlisle, now took place. The bedraggled express eventually reached its destination at around 4 in the morning after following the West Coast line via Carstairs, and yet another reversal from former Caledonian to North British lines in the Dalry/Haymarket area of the city.

Up express traffic had got through the Dunbar-Berwick stretch before midday, but it was thought prudent to divert the 10.37 Edinburgh-Leeds to the Waverley Route by combining it with the 10.10 to St. Pancras. By lunchtime, the West Coast line was being utilized, the 'Queen of Scots' Pullman not touching Edinburgh at all, with a connecting service being run to Carstairs.

'It may be years before the bridges can be rebuilt,' BR told the press. All Edinburgh-London expresses were immediately diverted via Carstairs, involving even the so-called non-stop 'Flying Scotsman' in a halt within 2 miles of starting in the up direction to reverse twice to reach former Caledonian metals. An obvious alternative would have been to reintroduce Edinburgh portions to Euston-Glasgow (Central) services with a stop to attach or detach vehicles at Carstairs or Symington. However, the need to conserve Tyneside's connections with Scotland—or possibly the rigidity of pre-nationalization management structures—meant that former LNER routes would be reopened as soon as possible. It added up to an unprecedentedly busy time in store for the Tweed Valley line!

From 16 August the Waverley Route and the line via Kelso were passable in one direction, with single-line working on both stretches. The 19.50 ex-Waverley was the first to use this route, and by the following day it was decided that all East Coast traffic would do so, bringing to an end the daily sight of the 'Scotsman' topping Beattock, and, on some days, Aisgill as well. An emergency timetable formalized the diversions from 23 August, and local bus services were introduced to operate out of Berwick, Dunbar and St Boswells.

In our age of HSTs and electric traction, where locomotive power is concentrated at a motorman's fingertips, it is difficult to envisage what this enforced diversion meant for long-distance train services. Expresses in those days were invariably loaded to near the 500 ton mark, and although timings were not tight, at a time when the railway system was still recovering from the neglect of the war years, the new route between Edinburgh and London was dauntingly difficult to operate.

Within 20 miles of leaving Edinburgh, London-bound trains faced around 10 miles of gradients averaging 1 in 75 to the 900-foot summit of Falahill, with the Eskbank curves to the north of the bank cutting out any real prospect of a fast approach. A banking engine was available from Hardengreen Junction if required. Northbound services had an easier climb, although still longer and harder than anything south of Berwick. Water could be taken at Galashiels, before the Waverley Route was left by up services at Kelso Junction, south of St Boswells, and here a new operational problem presented itself. The line from here to Kelso was not only single but subject to a 25 mph speed restriction; up to 45 mph was permitted on the former NER section east of Kelso, and water was available at Tweedmouth. It was expected that trains to and from destinations on the ECML would take water here or at Galashiels, as the nearest water-troughs were some 18 miles south of Tweedmouth, at Lucker.

Yet these obstacles failed to prevent the longest non-stop runs being made in Britain, indeed in Europe, by steam power. On no fewer than 17 occasions, beginning on 24 August, Britain's longest non-stop service, the 'Flying Scotsman', extended its normal 393-mile run to fully 408.65 miles, Falahill and the single-line Tweed Valley section included.

It was a masterly series of performances by men and machine, involving careful nursing of the injectors, and the courage to take a calculated risk in attacking Falahill's 900-foot summit knowing that any enforced stop on the climb would probably see the train stranded on the gradient until assistance could be summoned. Nor was it exclusively an achievement by the Haymarket crewmen responsible for operating the 'non-stop' north of York. While their King's Cross colleagues were riding 'on the cushions' when the emergency diversion was being traversed (crews were relieved through the unique corridor tender at the halfway stage of the non-stop journey in Yorkshire), they nevertheless had to exercise care in husbanding water and coal on the easier, but faster, stretches to the south. In other words, this was a superb example of grass-roots railway operation at its best; no official or manager ordered that these non-stop runs be performed during the emergency period. It was a triumph for the British railwayman refusing to be beaten by the elements.

\*     \*     \*

Freight was rolling again on the Scottish section of the East Coast Main Line by October 1948, and the 'Flying Scotsman', no longer

*Although connected with the Tweed Valley line at Roxburgh Junction, Jedburgh was also intended to be a branch terminus off the Border Counties line, when that cross-Border route was proposed to connect with the Waverley Route north of Hawick. However, the NBR always planned to reach 'Jeddart' from the north, but built its terminus rather far from the town. Not surprisingly, when passenger services were curtailed by the August 1948 floods, a taxi sufficed to take passengers to the junction! In this 1959 shot, 'D34' 4-4-0 No 62471* Glen Falloch *prepares to leave with an enthusiasts' special. (W. S. Sellar)*

non-stop in the winter timetable, was able to return to the route by 1 November. Branch services on the St Boswells-Duns and Jedburgh branches were not so lucky, being permanently withdrawn from the date of that not-so-glorious 'Twelfth'. Bus services substituting for the latter branch service proved to be needlessly over-capacity; a taxi soon sufficed until the formal withdrawal of the service.

Eight years later the Tweed Valley again played host to the Edinburgh-London 'non-stop' express, by now named the 'Elizabethan', when more torrential flooding closed the East Coast Main Line. Again, it happened in August, this time towards the end of the month (28th), and the 'Elizabethan' was the last southbound express to make it through the morass of the central Borders. Following trains—the 'Flying Scotsman' and its relief—attempted to follow the Waverley Route south from Edinburgh only to be turned back because of flooding near Melrose. The West Coast Main Line now had to be followed, and one of these expresses was seen in the Clyde Valley some 45 miles out from Edinburgh fully 5 hours after leaving! Two days later traffic returned to the East Coast after the water had gone down and some 200 tons of rubble cleared from the track.

Nor were these to be the last occasions when the line between Dunbar and Berwick made diversions necessary. In 1979 the author made a journey from Edinburgh to Newcastle which included disembarking from a train to a number of road coaches at Dunbar. This was because of the collapse of the tunnel at Penmanshiel, an

accident which had tragically cost the lives of three men. The road interlude was made memorable by the singing of drunken passengers (this was barely ten o'clock in the morning) but at Berwick they retired to the buffet car of the waiting HST, leaving this author to enjoy his first experience of High Speed Travel.

The road diversion was necessary because of the lack of any nearby alternative through railway, and the vulnerability of the line over Cockburnspath to the vagaries of the weather gods should perhaps have made BR hesitate about closing such a useful alternative—by 1979 the Tweed Valley had been closed to passengers (ie local services) for some 14 years. By the mid-1950s there had only been three passenger trains each way between Berwick (involving engine reversal at Tweedmouth) and St Boswells on the Waverley Route, plus three from the latter point to and from Kelso. As a schoolboy, the author saved up his pocket-money and made a special journey to sample the Tweed Valley services for himself in 1960, being disappointed to discover a 'V1' or 'V3' (who could ever tell the difference without measuring the coal bunker?) hauling the train—this class of 2-6-2 tank was of course commonplace in my own home town of Edinburgh. My (quite unjustifiable) hopes of seeing vintage NBR 4-4-0 power were dashed, while the last 'G5' 0-4-4 tank had long departed.

It was a line where former North Eastern and North British locomotives could often be seen working side by side. After 1924, when the former NBR roundhouse shed at Berwick closed, the eastern end of the Tweed Valley route was serviced by Tweedmouth, which also operated the line branching off from Coldstream to Wooler, as well as the entirely Scottish Burnmouth-Eyemouth and Reston-St Boswells branches.

Such a motley collection of branches and minor cross-country lines guaranteed a varied selection of locomotive deployment over the years, with Tweedmouth traditionally receiving a succession of 'hand-me-down' engines from NER depots, mainly on Tyneside. Tank engines were conspicuously, though not exclusively, to the fore along the Tweed, one such being a Fletcher 'BTP' 0-4-4 No 273 of the North Eastern Railway, which operated from the sub-shed of Sprouston for many years. One of the most interesting locomotives introduced between the wars was former Raven 'Pacific' tank engine No 2160 (LNER numbering), now converted to a 4-4-4T and stationed at Duns. It frequently worked over the Tweed line, in company with other NER types such as 'J25' 0-6-0s and 'D20' 4-4-0s, particularly on the eastern section. The LNER introduced a Sentinel railcar on the branch, while an 0-4-0 shunting engine from the same company operated at Kelso for around a quarter of a century. This was LNER No 8138, employed to relieve shunting horses in the Kelso yards, notorious for their short sidings. The 'main line' through Kelso was scarcely much easier to operate, westbound trains having to start on a 1 in 72 gradient.

However, it appears that little effort was made to co-ordinate through services. Of the five daily services westwards from Berwick in 1910, only three made reasonable connections with St Boswells trains, and none involved less than a 30-minute wait at Kelso. Indeed, a traveller on the 11.30 out of Berwick would reach Kelso in exactly an hour, but then have to await NBR connections at 14.00 or even 17.03. In the other direction, nothing better than a 45-minute wait at Kelso could be hoped for.

Operating factors made the Berwick-Kelso service over the Border slightly longer than it need have taken. Services from Berwick crossed the Royal Border Bridge southwards before the locomotive reversed direction and headed momentarily northwards, then west along the Tweed. Nevertheless, the 1910 timetable shows as little as 8 to 10 minutes being allowed between Berwick and Tweedmouth departure times; a 1955 traveller (C. J. B. Sanderson) joined a well-filled short train southbound out of Berwick behind an ex-NBR 'C16' tank only to find that most of the passengers got out at Tweedmouth! He described the operation of transferring to the Tweed Valley branch as involving running southwards through the station to a point opposite the locomotive depot, with the locomotive then running round the train and drawing into the down platform which apparently served branch traffic from both directions. The accompanying photograph by Mr John Robertson shows a 'G5' drawing a branch train off the main line, probably carrying out this very operation; the lack of a lampcode may be forgetfulness on the crew's part, to be rectified before the locomotive, probably still bearing a lamp on its bunker up to this point, led the train westwards. Any inconvenience resulting to the public from all this was probably compensated for by the bonus of having a through train from the Kelso area terminating at Berwick as well as serving Tweedmouth.

In July 1920 another reversing manoeuvre, this time at Roxburgh Junction, was the subject of a complaint by Jedburgh Town Council to the Ministry of Transport. 'Jeddart' travellers on the 09.31 out of their town were incensed by the fact that the train, after reversal at Roxburgh Junction where no less than 9 minutes were spent, reached Kelso 3 minutes *after* the departure of the 10.00 to Berwick. Similarly, the 18.48 westwards out of Kelso was perversely timed to depart 7 minutes *before* the arrival of a North Eastern 'connecting' train from Berwick.

The NBR's General Manager demanded an explanation from the Operating Department, whose Superintendent, C. H. Stemp, argued that recasting the timetable would cause 'considerable upset' and pointed out that existing services were geared to the comings and goings of main line trains at St Boswells and Tweedmouth. The 18.48 ex-Kelso, for example, could not be held for the 18.55 arrival from the east as this would make it late in connecting with the 18.05 Edinburgh-Carlisle at St Boswells. But why a 9 minute wait at Roxburgh on the 9.31? The Superintendent replied, when the Town

*Motive power for Berwick-Tweedmouth-Kelso passenger trains was still being provided by the 'G5' 0-4-4Ts of the former North Eastern Railway in the mid-1950s. Here, lacking a headlamp code, No 67248 appears to be bringing its Kelso-bound train off the main East Coast Main Line and into the down platform at Tweedmouth, after running round the stock. This locomotive was withdrawn in December 1958 after 64 years of service, although Tweedmouth had lost its allocation two years earlier. (John Robertson)*

Council pressed the point, that the locomotive had to run round its train but could not occupy the Roxburgh-Kelso section until it was vacated by a westbound service giving the Jedburgh passengers an immediate connection to St Boswells and points north and south. No consideration appears to have been given to starting the Kelso-St Boswells and Jedburgh-Kelso services 15 and 10 minutes earlier respectively to allow these connections to be made for both east- and west-bound passengers. It was a depressing episode of negative thinking; of running a railway for the convenience of its staff and not the public.

While through traffic could not be expected to be heavy, it could not possibly have harmed the railway companies' revenues to have ensured reasonable connections—or even to have worked through trains on a reciprocal basis. It would surely have benefited the NBR to do so, since this would have opened up tourist possibilities in an area the company was actively touting as 'The land of Scott'. Since the NBR owned both Berwick and Kelso stations, it would appear to have been in a particularly strong position to suggest more positive timetabling, but the lengthy sojourns at Kelso persisted into BR days, when the excuse of inter-company rivalry was no longer valid.

There were four stopping trains running throughout between St Boswells and Tweedmouth in the early 1950s (reduced to three from 1955), taking anything from 95 to 130 minutes for the 30-odd miles. One even stopped at Kelso for 54 minutes! It was the familiar story of a poorly-timed, grudgingly-offered rural train service receiving precisely the public reaction it deserved. It has to be admitted that the stations were not conveniently placed for the towns they nominally served, those of Carham and Coldstream, as we have seen, being in a different country, while Kelso citizens had to cross the river and address a fairly steep hill before the station was reached.

Despite the inconvenient locations of the line's stations—particularly Kelso's—as a powerful inhibitor to local use, BR did at one time attempt to stimulate through traffic between Edinburgh and Kelso. The 1961 timetable shows a DMU rostered to make a 2½ hour run from Waverley at 17.05 (via Peebles) accomplishing a mere 5 minute turnaround at Kelso, the St Boswells-Kelso section taking only 20 minutes eastbound and 2 minutes less in the other direction.

By 1964, the year of its closure, the St Boswells-Kelso-Berwick line's annual operating cost for passenger trains was £58,920 against receipts of £2,260, with an average number of six passengers per train. Yet the last train, headed by BR '2MT' No 78048, was seen off from the station on the evening of 13 June 1964 with a fusillade of detonators and a previously unknown soubriquet of 'Kelso Laddie' being bestowed on it by the local paper. Freight traffic continued to cross the Border at Carham until 29 March 1965, while the section west of Kelso survived for a further three years.

But it was perhaps BR's failure to encourage tourist traffic in an attractive and historic area that constituted such a waste of a useful transport resource, particularly if taken with the tragic loss of the northern part of the Waverley Route in 1969. As discussed in the chapter on that line, the Waverley Route could probably have been saved as far south as Hawick, had a different campaign been fought by local authorities and railway enthusiasts; BR might well have found it prudent to retain the line through Kelso for emergency diversions, instead of having closed it as a through route in 1965. From that hypothesis, who knows? Perhaps 'Dalesman'-type trains of the kind so successful (at the time of writing) on the present-day Settle and Carlisle could have been introduced along the banks of the Tweed, or possibly the area would have been fertile ground for a preservation initiative.

Wishful thinking, doubtless, but a 1980 survey of transport habits (see Bibliography under Hillman, Meyer) in the Newtown St Boswells area, at the western end of the Tweed Valley line, found that, rather than use road transport to Berwick-on-Tweed where HST links with London were available, local residents were simply finding other long-distance travel options. In other words, the line's potential as a feeder route for an area without its own route to the south was never apparently considered before closure took place.

\* \* \*

The author's last contact with the former Tweed Valley line was as a walker. Tramping nearly all of the St Boswells-Roxburgh Junction section of trackbed and between Coldstream and Sprouston gave little hint that here was once a highway on which streamlined steam locomotives, each of 150 tons, hauled lengthy trains three to four times their own weight between the English and Scottish capitals without a single stop. Few buildings or items of lineside equipment were left behind by the demolition contractors; on some lengths, the Tweed Valley line has now been incorporated into, and is indistinguishable from, adjoining fields.

# DEADWATER

## Border Counties

A cross-Border sign from the Border Counties line is now to be seen in the National Railway Museum at York. It was originally sited on the down side at Deadwater, and 32 years after the line's closure, the author and his wife visited the area to photograph the site where the line crossed between England and Scotland.

The previous day had produced incredible weather for the time of year—gale-force winds and lashings of rain. While we stood on the partly-flooded trackbed, flanked by overflowing ditches, we re-examined the map and the print of the accompanying 1956 photograph, so kindly provided by Mr Ian S. Carr. Suddenly, a clump of rushes beside the trackbed erupted into motion and a startled hind galloped past us and across the moorland. As city-dwellers we were thrilled to see such a large wild animal in such proximity, and its sudden appearance prompted me to look more carefully at the site. So badly flooded were the ditches on the up side, as well as parts of the trackbed itself, that a flow of water was detectable—there were in fact two miniature currents, going in opposite directions. We were at the watershed; a blade of grass or twig tossed into the ditch might find itself swept either north-westwards into the valleys drained by the Liddel and Esk and then out to the Solway, or south-eastwards into the drainage system of the North Tyne and eventually (in theory anyway) past Newcastle, the target for the North British in supporting and then taking over the Border Counties line.

Unusually, in fact almost uniquely, the railway itself represented the Anglo-Scottish Border for about 300 yards at Deadwater, the unseen frontier joining the trackbed from the north-east and then running due south in the up direction of the line before turning westwards again just before the station platform. There were at one time two sidings going off here; one is still visible in the 1958 picture of the station taken by Mr Douglas Hume, while the other connected

**Right** *The Border sign on the down side of the line at Deadwater on the Border Counties, photographed from a train in July 1956. It can now be seen at the National Railway Museum at York.* (Ian S. Carr)

**Far right** *Deadwater station, only just on the English side of the Border on the former Border Counties Railway. This picture was taken in September 1958, nearly two years after closure to passengers.* (Douglas Hume)

**Far right** *The Border sign on the up side of the Border Counties line at Deadwater, the only 'train' on this occasion, 7 September 1958, an engineer's vehicle. The line visible in the foreground was a short branch to Fairloans Quarry. Close to the down side of the line was a mineral well believed to have therapeutic properties – but Deadwater never became the Bath or Harrogate of the Border Counties!* (Douglas Hume)

with Fairloans Quarry about a quarter of a mile away on the hillside to the west. Interestingly, the 1925 Ordnance Survey map shows the existence of a 'sulphureous' well quite close to the down side of the station and even a bathing house. An odd place to come for a cure.

But enough of such musings. One of the most unremunerative railways ever built, the Border Counties line left the unique railway 'colony' of Riccarton on the Waverley Route and crossed into England between Saughtree and Deadwater. It eventually wended its way to Hexham, and, operated by the North British, offered that company the opportunity of a 'back door' route into Newcastle upon Tyne. This was bought at an enormously high price, resulting in the NBR contesting its own agreement in no fewer than 11 arbitration hearings.

The station at Deadwater was unusual in being managed by a stationmistress in the post-war years, and its closure probably increased the immediate population by some 50 per cent. Since there were only two houses there to begin with, the conversion of the station house to a private dwelling gave a massive proportional boost to the area's population! Obviously, to have built a branch line into the upper reaches of the North Tyne made little or no sense. The construction of a main line through the area might have succeeded if it was suitable for high speeds, much in the way that the Settle-Carlisle line, whatever its fate in the near future, offered more than a century of inter-city travel at reasonable timings. The Border Coun-

ties line was never going to do that.

On the last day of passenger services on the Border Counties Railway, Saturday 13 October 1956, so many wished to travel on the trains that the 11.10 to Hawick left Newcastle (Central) with six packed coaches and two more had to be coupled on at Hexham. 'If only,' mused last-day traveller Michael Robbins, 'a few more of these people had come for the trains before this day, they might not be having to come now.'

Yet even the most committed railway enthusiast would encounter difficulty in justifying a line through the valley of the North Tyne. The area north of Redesmouth (or Reedsmouth as the railway called it) was one of the most barren and least populated in Britain south of the Great Glen. Taxis, not even buses, were considered sufficient transport carriers to replace the trains, so small were the numbers involved! Not for the last time, we can only see this as evidence that railway companies—and particularly the long-sighted North British—were prepared to forego intermediate traffic receipts in staking a claim on a faraway target destination.

\*    \*    \*

As early as 2 October 1845 the North British Railway Directors, whose company had not opened a yard of track, were toying with the idea of a cross-Border line through the Cheviots. At that time the target was Newcastle, or even Darlington.

Interestingly, the idea for this seems to have come, not from Edinburgh, but from Darlington itself, where one of the Directors of the Stockton & Darlington and the newly-authorized Wear Valley Railways, John Castell Hopkins, addressed a NBR Board meeting to elicit interest in a route which would connect Edinburgh with his area by one shorter than the nascent East Coast line. The Board Minutes record that

'already railways exist between Darlington and Frosterly which can be advantageously used . . . and (he) produced plans of a survey which had been made by the Wear Valley Company from Frosterly to Haydon Bridge on one hand, and to near Haltwhistle on the other . . . it would be for the interest of this company, that a direct line should be made from some point on the Great North of England Railway near to or beyond Darlington to join with the Hawick Branch of this Railway, so as to give the shortest communication with London.'

The North British took this proposal seriously enough to immediately dispatch their Chairman, Vice-Chairman, Secretary and one other Director to Darlington for a conference with the idea's promoters. This meeting seems to have been hampered by the lack of engineering or surveying information available, and both sides agreed to await this data. By the end of the year the Wear Valley directors appear to have shelved their northwards extension for the current Parliamentary session, and little more was heard of this particular idea.

It had, however, raised a spectre which was to haunt North British consciousness for decades to come; a central route to Northern England.

In the following year the NBR was entertaining proposals from the Newcastle, Edinburgh & Glasgow Railway for a line between those three cities by way of Jedburgh, which was already a target destination for the Edinburgh Company as a branch terminus. In August 1846 the North British agreed to bear one-third of the surveying costs of such a line jointly with the NE & G and the new Great Northern Company. However, within a month the NBR cancelled its participation on hearing that the GNR was not in fact involved in the promotion.

On 11 December 1855 a first-sod-cutting ceremony took place at Tyne Green, Hexham. From this point the famous River Tyne divided, the South Tyne providing the Newcastle & Carlisle Railway with a pass towards the west, while its northern counterpart drained the foothills of the Cheviots. The symbolic cutting at this location was carried out by W. H. Charlton, Chairman of the Border Counties Railway, which was intended to bring rails to the North Tyne valley and link up with the North British in southern Scotland.

At this time the NBR, anxious to reach Carlisle as well as keep open any means of approaching Newcastle by a 'back door' route, was looking to extend its Edinburgh-Hawick branch southwards, although its route, originally planned via Teviotdale and Langholm, was apparently irretrievably blocked by the Caledonian Railway. In any event, this route was not at all convenient for any approach towards the North Tyne. In obtaining authorization in 1854 for their line from Hexham to Kielder, the BCR Directors unknowingly altered the entire structure of cross-Border railways, deprived Langholm of a through rail service, and created one of the most fascinating and unremunerative railways it would be possible to imagine.

Yet a Border Counties prospectus issued in November 1857 for the 'Extension into Scotland' summarized the company's earlier plans, and these included a northwards route through Knot-i-the-gate and the valley of the Rule Water to join with the North British near Belses (*north* of Hawick). Plans deposited with the local authorities exactly one year earlier showed that the Border Counties northern extension into Scotland was even more ambitious in scope than finally constructed.

As envisaged by engineers John F. Tone and Francis Charlton, the 32-mile line from Belling would have crossed the Border at Deadwater, but thereafter taken a more northerly direction. Knot-i-the-gate might have given its romantic name to a famous railway tunnel, for here there would have been a 1,380-yard bore with the summit of the line at its southern portal. To reach this point, trains travelling northwards would have climbed 5 miles at 1 in 100 with hardly a break, but this pales into insignificance compared to the summit's Scottish approach. *Fifteen* miles up from Tempendean at a ruling gradient of 1 in 100, with a few easier stretches, would have been an incline to rival Whitrope, and with the final ¾ mile in tunnel!

In case the reader is bemused by all this into thinking that intermediate traffic might make such enterprise worthwhile, rest assured that Knot-('Note' in the 1856 plans)-i-the-gate makes even Deadwater look metropolitan. When the author recently motored over what the BCR planned as its hard-earned summit, not a single habitation was to be glimpsed through the low-lying clouds.

A north-facing junction gave rise to a 2½-mile Jedburgh branch, the junction's direction ensuring that a double reversal would be necessary for any traffic intended for nearby Hawick from the branch. In any event, it appears from the plans that the branch terminus was not actually located in Jedburgh itself.

At Belses Mill, north of Hawick on the NBR line, a south-facing junction must have rung alarm bells in Edinburgh 44 miles away. No rail plans for southern Scotland projected by English-based business-men and speculators could leave the North British unconcerned—this could easily have been a Trojan Horse with the North Eastern inside. Not too surprisingly, given this (surely unjustified) concern (after all, the NER was already at Kelso), the North British man-oeuvred itself into a deadlocked position.

Although the company Minutes of the time are not specific on the point, the NBR's attitude to the northward-thrusting Border Counties Railway was inextricably linked with the Edinburgh company's own attempts to convert its existing, unremunerative, Hawick branch into a through Anglo-Scottish route. Prevented from building its own Hawick-Carlisle line via Langholm by the Caledonian's supporters in Parliament in 1847—in fact, the company's finances would almost certainly have prohibited any such construction anyway—the NBR was left at Hawick gazing at the Cheviots separating it from English traffic. Matters were made worse by the Caledonian obtaining permission to build a line over the self-same route via Langholm, so the best the NBR could hope for would be some kind of joint line, and with no guarantee of 'Caley' co-operation—after all, that com-pany already had an Edinburgh-Carlisle line. All this is discussed in the next chapter on the Waverley Route, but it is not difficult to see that the NBR directors must have viewed the BCR as a viable option, even if it meant building southwards from Hawick via Riccarton and Newcastleton in order to command a second route to England via the North Tyne as well as Carlisle. What is remarkable, looking back with hindsight, is the enthusiasm with which the North British settled for this option. It was to cost them dear.

Not surprisingly, the Border Counties Directors in late 1857 enthused about the new plan to reach the NBR much further south, at Riccarton—a 14-mile extension for them instead of 30 miles. 'This will prove a highly remunerative investment,' the investors were told. John Thomas records that Charlton was friendly with the NBR chairman, Richard Hodgson, and they obviously believed that the

North Tyne extension would be mutually beneficial.

Indeed, by the summer of 1860 the two companies were amalgamated. By this time, the North British had received the go-ahead to build to Carlisle via Riccarton and appears to have taken an active part in constructing the Border Counties from Riccarton to Thorneyburn; £20,000 was budgeted for this by the NBR in 1859. The southern section of the BCR appears to have been operated by the NB even before amalgamation, and long before there was any physical means of contact between the two railway companies.

Early in 1859 the Parliamentary committee investigating the Hawick-Carlisle line learned that the BCR had £127,000 in paid-up capital with another £112,000 to come from stock calls. Yet the North British Minutes suggest that the northern extension of the BCR would cost an enormous £286,000 (the line to Carlisle was costed at £339,000). Against this, the North British believed that some £16,343 worth of traffic would feed annually into their system, generated by the Border Counties connection. This was less than one-third of the turnover of London-Edinburgh passenger traffic by the East Coast route the previous year. When freight is allowed for in the projected turnover figure for the Border Counties, where was the logic in seeing the BCR as any kind of long-distance trunk line, unless traffic was to be generated locally, and where was that to come from?

*   *   *

The resulting line was opened in successive sections over a total of some 6½ years, a rate of progress—barely 7 miles per year—indicating the engineering and fund-raising problems involved. Riccarton was not reached until the summer of 1862, and it appears that services began while some of the works were still incomplete, a sure sign that revenue was desperately needed. H. A. Vallance records that a Beyer Peacock 2-2-2 No 216 (later 1006) was used on the line from the first, amassing over a million miles up to 1912. Other North British stalwarts on the Border Counties included the Wheatley 4-4-0 No 224 which went down with the first Tay Bridge but was resurrected to run on the Border lines under the grim nickname of 'The Diver', but later NBR 4-4-0s were to be seen on the line up to the time of closure.

If comparatively little has been recorded about this uncommercial but fascinating line, the same cannot be said of the community at its north end, at Riccarton Junction. Here the North British built a township to support the necessary locomotive and permanent way facilities established in the wilds of Roxburghshire where the Waverley Route and Border Counties line divided at the south end of the island platform, complete with narrow bay. Interestingly, the locomotive shed was not built straight away, until the NBR found that 100 route-miles of light engine running was being notched up daily between Riccarton and Hawick in the first summer of operation.

But Riccarton was more than just a station and junction. This was

**Above** *Class '26' diesel D5317 pulls into Riccarton with a Carlisle-Edinburgh stopping train on the last day of operation on the Waverley Route, Saturday 4 January 1969. The station buildings had double functions, with a shop being housed among the offices. (W. S. Sellar)*

**Right** *Riccarton village was about to be abandoned for the last time when this picture was taken on the same day. Class '55' 'Deltic' No D9002 The King's Own Yorkshire Light Infantry is seen leaving Riccarton on a northbound enthusiasts' special over the Waverley Route. By this time the Border Counties branch had ceased to exist for more than ten years. (W. S. Sellar)*

*Riccarton Junction from the south, with the Border Counties line, which has just crossed into Scotland at nearby Deadwater, entering the foreground of the picture. The Waverley Route enters from the south at the middle left and exits northwards near the signalbox at the top left. This view circa 1953 clearly shows the lean-to engine shed and the station with its bay.* (courtesy R. Clapperton)

as much a 'railway town' as Swindon or Crewe; more so, since for most if not all of its existence, this Roxburghshire community had no proper road access. Consequently its social services had to be provided by the railway company in a unique example of corporate paternalism.

Consisting of 33 houses (an increase of 19 on the original number planned in 1862), Riccarton grew to have a population of about 100. It was reported that no 'servants' houses' were available in September 1862, which was probably just as well, as a contract for gas lighting at the site was not given out until January 1863. The village's public utilities were located in the railway buildings. One of the first church sites was the locomotive shed, no doubt an unpopular venue for worshippers in their 'Sunday best'. Services were at first taken by a minister from Saughtree generously funded with a walking pass by the NBR. In later years a special Sunday train was instituted to take residents to Hawick and Newcastleton in alternate weeks.

The station buildings housed a Co-operative shop, with the waiting room including a Post Office counter. A refreshment room was franchised to a lady named Elizabeth Stule, whose Carstairs address suggests she was changing from one junction station to another even more isolated! She was to be accepted 'subject to enquiries about her means and character'. A primary school was specially built, but children of secondary school age travelled to Hawick in a coach attached to the 06.30 Carlisle-Edinburgh freight. Medical facilities consisted of a pilot engine maintained at readiness to bring a doctor from Newcastleton 8 miles away, when required. The very need for the railway company to be involved in such regular errands of mercy underlines the underdeveloped nature of the countryside in which the NBR and BCR were so determined to build their lines.

\*　　\*　　\*

The 1909-10 North British working timetable listed eight trains in the up, and six in the down, direction throughout the entire Border Counties line between Riccarton and Hexham. There were three through passenger services, the 16.51 (16.15 ex-Newcastle) in the down direction being described as an express, despite making 12 stops on its 93-minute traverse of this section of line! Two of the freight services were timetabled from Sighthill (Glasgow) to Newcastle (04.10 out of Riccarton) and a Portobello-Newcastle goods (17.20 from Riccarton).

In 1921 the NBR considered resuming its overnight freight workings between Glasgow and Tyneside over the BCR after the First World War, an operation which would obviously entail reintroducing a night shift. However, the Operating Superintendent, C. H. Stemp, suggested the introduction of Long Distance Tablet switching, so as to minimize signalling costs, calculating that although the

*Last day at Reedsmouth, 13 October 1956. 'K1' 2-6-0 No 62022 takes the Border Counties line for Riccarton with the last northbound service, the 11.10 ex-Newcastle, offering its enthusiast passengers the chance of a round trip from Tyneside and back via Carlisle. The southbound Carlisle connection had to be held specially at Riccarton for the 'Mogul' with its wreath-bedecked smokebox door. (John Robertson)*

reintroduction would cost £2,995, this would be £1,079 less than required for overnight operations before the First World War. Stemp's suggestion indicates that the Border Counties line was regarded by grass-roots railwaymen as worthy of investment and that it did, at that time, have an important part to play in the operation of the network.

By 1941 three through passenger trains were still being provided each way, in the up direction the 06.42, 10.20 and 16.53 out of Riccarton, the first and last of these being ex-Hawick. The fastest of these took 90 minutes for the 40¾ miles to Border Counties Junction, west of Hexham, the slowest requiring 104 minutes. Northwards, the 07.01, 12.04 and 17.12 out of Hexham (the first two having started at Newcastle) required anything from 97 to 110 minutes, the slower times reflecting the adverse gradients in this direction. The freights from Glasgow and Edinburgh to Tyneside appear to have been redirected from the East Coast Main Line by the LNER some time before this. In 1941 the line appears to have been worked in the following sections:

Riccarton (South) to Kielder

Kielder to Falstone

Falstone to Reedsmouth

(with a staffed signalbox at Bellingham)

Reedsmouth to Wark

Wark to Wall

Wall to Hexham (BC Junction)

The last official day of scheduled operations, 13 October 1956, saw regular passenger services end in chaos. Apparently the Saturdays only 10.39 Hexham-Kielder was held at Border Counties Junction for 50 minutes owing to a tablet failure. This affected the southbound running of the 10.22 out of Riccarton, hauled by '3MT' 2-6-0 No 77011, which could not progress south of Reedsmouth until 13.06, reaching Hexham 100 minutes late. With so much single track, it was inevitable that the 11.10 out of Newcastle would be adversely affected much to the chagrin of its Tyneside-based enthusiasts anxious to secure a connection at Riccarton for Carlisle, and thus complete a round journey. The packed weight of the eight-coach train would hardly ease the job for the 'K1' in charge, and it was with considerable relief that the travellers came into sight of Riccarton, complete with an 'A3' 'Pacific' waiting with a southbound connection!

But all this did not in fact see the complete end of the line. Surprisingly, a DMU comprising an Institute of Transport special visited Kielder on 29 May 1957, and there were reports of military traffic on the line the following autumn, one such train being run from West Woodburn to Elgin—ten coaches hauled by 'K1' No 62030 giving way at Hawick to a 'K3' and 'B1' pairing. Ramblers' specials ran on the Border Counties both that year and in 1958, but complete closure came soon afterwards.

Nowadays much of the course and lineside area of the former

*The course of the Border Counties line looking northwards from Deadwater in July 1988. The trackbed at this point is the actual Anglo-Scottish border, the railway once running between Scotland (left) and England (right) for about a quarter of a mile. (Author)*

*The author standing on the trackbed between Deadwater and Saughtree. The thistles on the right of the picture are appropriate vegetation, considering that the former railway had just crossed into Scotland at this point. (M. Mullay)*

*A bufferstop on the England-Scotland border; the abandoned trackbed stretches northwards into the distance. Deadwater station, still extant, is immediately behind the cameraman. (Author)*

Border Counties Railway has changed out of all recognition; indeed, part of it is no longer on the map. South of Kielder village the line's course plunges into the waters of Bakethin reservoir, just north of its even larger Kielder counterpart. The latter is the largest man-made lake in Europe, and the resulting tourist and recreational facilities centred on it are well served by a new road from the south. Huge forests of conifers—Kielder at 40,000 acres is the biggest in northern England and Wark second only to it—have transformed the valley walls. The BCR's disappearance from the landscape of the valley has more than just a symbolic significance—the railway failed to make a lasting effect on the economy of the valley and the lifestyle of its inhabitants. It should surely never have been built, certainly not north of Bellingham and over the Border.

# KERSHOPEFOOT

# Waverley Route

*Kershopefoot (locally pronounced 'Kersipfoot') station photographed in mid-December 1968, only three weeks before closure. The view looks northwards towards the Scottish Border. Note the unusual lack of a footbridge.* (Douglas Hume)

Nowadays only foresters and agricultural workers tread across the Anglo-Scottish Border at Kershopefoot, where 12-wheeled monsters once hauled hundreds of tons of metal up Liddesdale towards Scotland's capital. Where the snail-like Admiralty leave-train of the First World War used to carry weary sailors to and from Scapa Flow past Kershopefoot, where once the luxurious Midland Pullman coaches blurred past, now there is only a cart-track.

Considering that Carlisle, one of the cities connected by the erstwhile Waverley Route, is only a few miles from the Border, it is remarkable that the actual crossing point for the line occurs some 21 miles from Carlisle's Citadel station. This was partly because of the NBR's somewhat circuitous route out of Carlisle, coupled with the topographical factors involved. (In fact, the Anglo-Scottish Border makes a short zigzag on to the Waverley Route south of Riddings junction, at Liddel Mote. This was not publicized by the NBR, LNER or BR, and is mentioned here only for accuracy's sake. The author is indebted to Mr. R. B. McCartney for this information.)

\*     \*     \*

The Waverley Route seems to have stimulated interest among railway enthusiasts out of all proportion to its commercial value. It achieved notoriety in 1969 by being the first British main line to be closed in almost its entirety, but it had an attraction of its own long before then. Now it rivals the nearby Dere Street, the main Roman road in the area, as an archaeological vestige of a transport facility of long ago.

The Waverley Route was first conceived on 27 June 1844 when the North British Railway Company empowered their engineer, John Miller,

*Kershopefoot 20 years later. Viewed from the site of the former level crossing, the Waverley Route trackbed stretches northward on the long climb to Whitrope.* (Author)

'to make a flying survey of the Country and to report as to the expediency of extending the Dalkeith Line to the South, and of this company taking the

Berwick and Kelso Line as a Branch and to state his views generally as to both measures'.

As discussed in the chapter on the East Coast Main Line, the North British made a crucial purchase of the Edinburgh & Dalkeith Railway in 1844-5, giving it immediate access to the Lothian coalfield and the ports of Leith and Fisherrow even before a continuous line of track was laid between Edinburgh and Berwick. The above quotation from the Board Minutes is an indication that the putative railway-makers were keen to widen their horizons, the Directors being told specifically at the same meeting that the purchase would allow access to Galashiels. The Berwick and Kelso line did not of course exist, even some 33 years after the Act of Parliament enabling it.

On 4 September the NBR Board ordered traffic studies to be carried out between Scotland's capital and the towns of Galashiels, Melrose and Peebles. Within a fortnight the scene had become more complicated by the emergence of a group of Galashiels-based promoters determined to connect their town with the Scottish capital. Led by Messrs Haldane and Bowie Stewart Campbell, the Galashiels contingent was taken very seriously by the NBR, who agreed to be bound by an agreement to guarantee building a 'first-class' passenger station there along with a 'depot for coals, lime, stone, timber and other articles', even if the NBR continued the line farther south. In return, the Galashiels businessmen allowed the NBR a free hand. The company also paid £1,200 for the expenses the promoters had already incurred for surveys, the results of these being transferred to the NBR.

While it seems possible that the sum paid was exorbitant—the acquisition of these survey plans did not relieve Miller of his task of surveying a route southwards—it was probably good public relations to pay for allies in Galashiels, which could conceivably be a logical operating centre for the central Borders, as indeed it became.

The Waverley Route, as it was later called, was not originally conceived as a cross-Border trunk line to rival those of East and West. Indeed, on 11 October 1844 a proposal to the NBR Board 'to extend the projected Galashiels Railway to Carlisle, was considered and negatived'. It was decided to build on to Hawick, however, despite an attempt by two important Directors (Christison and Cadell) to restrict this extension to Melrose only. At the same time, the decision was taken not to announce any intention of building a line from Berwick to Kelso.

Only eight days later the line south to the Borders again occupied the attention of men who had quite enough on their hands in building the line to Berwick. This time the NBR Directors considered a letter from the Glasgow, Dumfries & Carlisle Railway inviting them to join with that company in creating a trunk line between Carlisle and Edinburgh 'in the event of the Caledonian Railway being rejected' in its efforts to obtain parliamentary approval. The southern part of this line would be built by the GD & C from Carlisle to Hawick 'by the valley of the Esk'—a significant choice of route, one to be examined more closely later—to connect with the NBR's intended line.

Chairman Learmonth urged his fellow Directors to support the other Company's plan to approach the Board of Trade with this proposal, but for once, did not have it all his own way. John Christison, one of the directors who wanted the new southwards line to end at Melrose, never mind Hawick or Carlisle, moved an amendment that the NBR Directors 'cannot further extend the great responsibility they have already undertaken in agreeing to make the line from Edinburgh to Hawick'.

Nevertheless, despite Christison's opposition, the NBR shareholders were told, at the end of 1844, that there was in fact a possibility of linking at Hawick with the Glasgow, Dumfries & Carlisle, and the modern historian can only suspect that the Directors were erring on the side of over-pitching their request for support for the Hawick branch. After all, their main line to Berwick was not even scheduled to carry traffic until May 1846; now, as the Board Minutes put it, 'the directors are aware of the delicacy of bringing forward a proposal for so large an addition to the works of the Company at so early a period in their existence'.

Interestingly, economic historian C. J. A. Robertson believes that the NBR's 'willingness to leave the route (south of Hawick) to another group of projectors whose chances of authorization in the face of the Caledonian were at best doubtful suggests that they did not yet attach the highest priority to the Carlisle line'. Yet, within a year, Carlisle was very much a target destination within the Company's sights—it is probably true to say that the Board was itself split on the matter, and considerable vacillation of purpose is evident in the company records.

What was definitely being proposed was a 45-mile branch to Hawick, of which the first eight were already in existence, to be built at around £8,000 per mile. A single line was envisaged, the shareholders being told that this would be sufficient for through traffic, even if the Glasgow, Dumfries & Carlisle did reach Hawick. Six months later the NBR shareholders had convinced themselves that double track would be necessary—the Hawick line itself was to be double, a decision taken on 21 June 1845, although the Board of Trade appears to have insisted on this for future trunk line provision after the end of 1845. Any Anglo-Scottish traffic was honestly described as likely to be light; the 'west' of England, and not London, was the area described as being brought into contact with Edinburgh. (In contrast, the GD & C company saw themselves as an alternative to the Caledonian.)

It was as if the North British Directors were unable to decide between policies of caution and opportunism—there can have been few railway enterprises that were being promoted so half-heartedly for their projected traffic potential in what was rapidly turning into the age of the Railway Mania. At the same time, the NBR supporters were aware of the need to establish a line into a large area of virgin railway territory without alarming Hudson and other English supporters with the impression that here would be a rival line to the British capital.

In other words, what was to become the Waverley Route was not built as a main line between the English and Scottish capitals for the simple reason that it dare not be seen as one. It is no great surprise to learn that, early in 1845, Hudson's York & North Midland Railway expressed disapproval of the Hawick branch, whose strategic potential would not be lost on an experienced operator like Hudson.

By the summer of 1845 the North British was more sanguine towards its conquest of the Borders in the direction of Carlisle; a double-track line was now planned all the way to Carlisle. Raising capital of £800,000 would be split equally between NBR and (nominally independent) Edinburgh & Hawick Railway shareholders. The Hawick line already authorized would cost £13,000 per mile, 'there being no heavy works to execute'—so much for Falahill bank and the serpentine nature of the Gala Water, to say nothing of having to cross the Tweed south of Galashiels! New revenue calculations had boosted the line's theoretical earning capacity to £35,612 per annum. Again, there was no mention of a possible new route for London traffic; only the 'west' of England was stipulated.

Parliamentary approval being obtained for the Hawick branch, work on bringing rails to the Borders—a large area of which no longer has a single yard of track—began in the autumn of 1845. Early in that year, rivalry with the Caledonian had begun to sharpen the NBR's appetite for territory. An alliance 'to throw out the Caledonian Railway' was agreed with the Edinburgh & Glasgow, GD & C and Ayrshire Railways in February, with a joint purse of £30,000 for parliamentary and legal costs. At this stage, the NBR was prepared to lease any resulting line south from Hawick, and within a few months the shareholders were asked to approve a double line to that town, while, confusingly, the Board had not ruled out the company's own extension to Carlisle, with a branch to Canonbie.

With the Caledonian 'enemy' now proposing its Extension eastwards through the central Borders to the Tweed's mouth, at right-angles to the NBR's expansion southwards, the latter company was not slow in publicizing its intention to build branches in the area, a deputation being sent to various local burghs. In March 1845 surveys of lines to Kelso, Innerleithen and Duns were approved, while Jedburgh Town Council enthusiastically welcomed the NB's deputation. Curiously, the Peebles branch being proposed at this stage was to approach the town from the south, along the Tweed. The North British Directors appear to have seen the Tweed Valley as negotiable ground in their conflict with the Caledonian—the Board Minutes in September 1845 show that the Glasgow interloper would be tolerated as far as Innerleithen 'but no farther', but before the month was out the NBR was hinting to the Caledonian that it had its own plans to build a line westwards from Peebles towards Biggar in Lanarkshire, while offering to compromise on Peebles as a 'frontier'.

The idea of a NBR line to Biggar could never have been anything other than an empty threat, but it seems to have resolved the matter satisfactorily for the Company. On 2 February 1846, the Board was told that, following a conference between the respective Company representatives, Peebles would now be considered as a 'frontier' between the two systems in the Borders, the NBR surrendering any idea of advancing westwards from here towards Biggar, whence the Caledonian could build to Peebles. Ironically, not a yard of track had yet been built at or near Peebles; equally, today, not a yard of railway exists within 15 miles of this attractive town, once the target for so much intrigue between railway companies.

The same conference which decided on Peebles as a boundary for the respective NBR and Caledonian spheres of influence was in fact aborted as soon as the topic of the Hawick-Carlisle area was raised. The Caledonian refused even to discuss any question of the Edinburgh Company extending its line southwards to Carlisle—after all, it was within a few months of opening an East Coast route across the Border—and suggested that the NB build towards Gretna, an alternative the latter company refused to consider.

It was of course the NBR's intention to seek Parliamentary permission for exactly both these options included among four bills in the ensuing session—for branch lines in general, for branch lines specifically off the Hawick line, for an extension of this line to Carlisle, and finally for a branch from this extension to join the Caledonian at or near Springfield, a 'suburb' of Gretna (if such a thing is possible).

Not too surprisingly, the North British encountered opposition with the third and fourth of these proposals. After all, it was barely five years since a government commission had suggested that only one Anglo-Scottish route would suffice for the traffic anticipated; yet here was a company already well on the way to crossing the Border in the east with a rival scheme, it must have seemed, to the Caledonian's crossing in the west. By May 1846 the NBR was advised that there was a problem with the preamble to its Hawick-Carlisle bill, and early the following month, its bill failing, the Directors were considering asking the shareholders for permission to petition Parliament in the following session. The NBR's Board authorized a £1,000 payment to its parliamentary agents, despite this rebuff at Westminster, and at the same meeting ordered the locomotives for the Hawick line, their number to be decided on the advice of John Miller. (This was despite the fact that the NBR already had a locomotive superintendent, suggesting that the Edinburgh-Berwick and Edinburgh-Hawick enterprises were being kept administratively well apart at this time.) These engines were to be obtained at a price of £2,373 each, or less if their cost would be haggled downwards. Thirty rail carriages were ordered in July 1846. It was all to prove more than a little premature.

\* \* \*

Before going on to examine the early history of the line north of Hawick—destined to be the southern terminus of the Waverley Route until 1862—it is fascinating to examine Miller's conception of the Hawick-Carlisle line in 1846, as surveyed for the parliamentary bill which failed that year, compared with what was ultimately built south of Hawick.

In his university thesis listed in the Bibliography, modern writer John Elliot (a splendid Border name!) has illustrated the sound commercial factors which confirmed Miller's route via Langholm as the natural one south from Hawick. The town of Langholm, which should have enjoyed a direct main line connection with Edinburgh and Carlisle, but had to settle for being the terminus of a branch from Riddings Junction, produced more receipts than the principal main-line station in Liddesdale, the route eventually used to connect Hawick and Carlisle (more details can be found in the chapter on the Langholm branch). Not only would a Langholm route have made more commercial sense, but all the engineering factors pointed to a line through Teviotdale rather than the Liddesdale one eventually constructed.

Miller's plans of 1846 can still be seen in the Scottish Record Office (RHP44774) and they show a main line which would have been far more conducive to express train operation than the later route via Riccarton. South from Hawick the 41½ miles to Carlisle would have begun by running alongside the River Teviot to Mosspaul summit 817 feet above sea level, before threading a 300-yard tunnel at Eweslees and following a falling gradient to Langholm. South-east of there a facing branch came in from the coal-bearing area of Canonbie, before a 350-yard viaduct at Riddings. The line would have passed north of Longtown, while the planned Caledonian main line would have been joined and paralleled at Etterby. This would have been an exchange junction, the NBR then striking south-eastwards over the Eden towards its own terminal station in the part of Carlisle where Rickergate becomes Scotch Street. A potential deviation route would have brought the line into Carlisle in the shadow of the castle walls. Whether it would have made good sense to have its own station in the Border City is a quandary that the company was fortunate not to have to unravel.

As for gradients, trains following Miller's route between Hawick and Carlisle would have been saved some 175 feet of climbing, thanks to the lower height of the Mosspaul pass as compared to that at Limekilnedge (Whitrope to railway enthusiasts). From Hawick the 1846 line would have climbed 481 feet in 11¾ miles at a ruling gradient of 1 in 135, the toughest stretch being 1 in 90 for not more than 3 miles. Miller was not cheapskate with his bridges—the Teviot was to be crossed 13 times in 6 miles, just as his Edinburgh-Hawick line crossed the Gala Water no fewer than eight times in as many miles north of Galashiels. It would have been a highly scenic route, as a road journey on the present-day A7 will confirm (naturally the road sensibly takes the Mosspaul route).

Downhill from Mosspaul, slightly steeper gradients would have prevailed down to Langholm, averaging roughly 1 in 100, then 1¾ miles down at 1 in 80 would have eased to 1 in 148 through the tunnel, followed by 3½ at 1 in 90. (Incidentally, it would have been hard to beat the southern approach to the Mosspaul pass for grandeur of scenery; one wonders what O. S. Nock would have made of a footplate run northwards on the 'Waverley' express as his Gresley 'Pacific' prepared to attack the Mosspaul bank at speed!)

South of Langholm there would have been a tough 1½ miles at 1 in 75 before the Riddings viaduct was reached by northbound trains. There can be no doubt that the gradients designed by Miller would have been substantial, although not as bad as Whitrope taken from either north or south. Interestingly, the comparatively widespread location of the gradients would have probably necessitated banking assistance for freight trains from the Longtown area, and not just from Langholm. However, passenger trains, even those stopping at Langholm, would have had no difficulty in climbing this bank without assistance.

Meanwhile, work inched southwards from Edinburgh in the conquest of the Borders—and not without death stalking the steps of the railway-makers. By February 1846, two 10-mile sections were in the course of construction north and south of Fushiebridge, a now-vanished village to the south of Gorebridge. The more northern of these was manned by Irish navvies, the section south of it by a mixture of Scottish and English labourers. Relations between the two sets of men were not good and at the end of the month—payday—the area was to witness one of the most unpleasant incidents involving railway labourers in the whole United Kingdom.

It appears that, owing to the infamous 'tommy' system, the Irish workforce received less than they took to be their due that fateful Saturday and there were mutterings among the Irishmen as many of them drowned their sorrows in a Gorebridge inn. When a pedlar unwisely passed two watches around among them to negotiate sales, he found it necessary to call the constabulary to recover the timepieces, which had immediately gone missing. Unfortunately, in the turmoil that followed, two Irishmen were arrested, only to be released by a gun-packing mob of Irishmen who overcame the local police. Even worse than this, the triumphant navvies encountered two other officers attempting to hide from their approach and promptly bludgeoned one of them, Constable Richard Pace of the County Police, insensible. Neighbours carried him to his home nearby, but he died the following evening, leaving a widow.

This murder triggered a reaction from the Scottish and English navvies also in the area and approximately 1,000 of them decided to take the law into their own hands. After putting a force of Irishmen to flight at nearby Crichton, the enraged navvies destroyed the huts in which the Irish lived, apparently with the police looking on. Ironically, Irish dragoons were sent from Piershill barracks in Edinburgh to help restore order that weekend, and the local Sheriff was successful in stopping a counterforce of Irish labourers in advancing from Edinburgh to the scene. By the following Thursday both sets of navvies were back at work, while at Borthwick kirkyard the body of Constable Pace was laid to rest, a forgotten martyr to the inexorable progress of the railway.

While the Berwick line opened in the summer of 1846, the NBR was giving out contracts for the next sections of the Hawick line—a total of 31,000 yards to be prepared at Heriot, Stow, Minto and Hawick. In September the sites of the Galashiels, Melrose and St Boswells stations were fixed by a visiting committee of Directors, the first two of these sites being well-placed near the centre of their respective towns.

It does not require mathematical genius to calculate that the Hawick branch took longer to construct, per mile, than the Edinburgh-Berwick line. Despite construction starting late in 1845, no train ran on the new line for three years, and then for only part of the way. Indeed, the 52-mile line nearly brought the company to its knees.

Early in 1848 the NBR found it necessary to raise a further loan of £35,000 to try to take the railway to Galashiels, only some 33 miles from the Capital, and that was before estimates had been sought for the digging of Bowshank tunnel, to the north of the town. Obviously, the new line into the Borders was costing more than had been anticipated, the Borthwick embankment proving to be a major construction. By the December of the year, with freight trains running on the line, but only as far as the still incomplete tunnel, the Directors were having to borrow another £150,000 on their own personal security.

By the end of 1848 the railway company was in crisis. So bad were economic conditions generally that shareholders were failing to answer for their commitments towards capital (arrears stood at £270,182 in November), and with the Borders line making slow progress, and the shipowners slashing their rates to make a successful counter-attack on the NBR's Berwick line traffic, it is small wonder that in October 1848 the Directors were having to go cap in hand to George Hudson to seek an amalgamation or at least the leasing of the Berwick line by his York, Newcastle & Berwick company. In April of that year the Board had optimistically authorized stations (similar to Burnmouth's) for Tynehead, Heriot, Stow and Fountainhall, and 'resolved to proceed with the works to St Boswells with as much expedition as the financial affairs of the Company will allow', but by the turn of the year could only decide on the option of 'going on slowly as at present, and indeed rather to stop any of the works not imperatively required if it can be done without damage or loss'.

In particular it was decided on 16 November not to proceed with work south of St Boswells for the time being (bridging the Tweed north of Melrose was estimated at nearly £5,000), and when it was resumed there was to be no line-building into Hawick south or west of the turnpike road into the town. This was to avoid the heavy claims of a particular landowner, possibly the adventurist Town Council itself, although the NBR had already bought part of the Common Haugh on the west bank of the Teviot. This would have given a very central station site, and trains arriving from Edinburgh would have been pointing towards the Mosspaul pass. Cutting back to the north of the town was not just a saving, it must have made it easier to decide on an alternative Slitrig/Liddesdale route to the south when that was ultimately sought. There is no hint of any such motive in the NBR's archives at the time; had the recession not occurred, to prevent the building of a more central Hawick station, one wonders if the cost-conscious NBR would have been so happy to build anew on a station site north of the river so as to expedite a line climbing south-eastwards up the valley of the Slitrig Water to Whitrope. As it was, the Hawick station was costed at approximately £1,958 including an iron roof. A large turntable, presumably for locomotives, was ordered for Hawick at £300.

Trains finally reached there in November 1849, the station building being hung with evergreens and flags in celebration. Interestingly, this building with its three tracks, plus one immediately to the south, was later redesignated the goods shed, its position confirming that the layout of Hawick station was originally polarized towards a southwards continuation along the western bank of the Teviot and then on towards the Border via Mosspaul.

\*     \*     \*

Ten years later, on 7 September 1859, a public holiday was called in Hawick. Despite heavy rain, a sod-cutting ceremony took place at Lynwood—later to be the site of a spectacular viaduct over the Slitrig Water—and the town celebrated the beginning of the Border Union Railway extension from Hawick to Carlisle—via Whitrope.

It was a desperately bad choice of route. Not only was it going to involve considerable engineering difficulties—in contrast to the sanguine, if not downright inaccurate, information supplied by its promoters—but it was commercially questionable from the start. Why then, were the Hawick citizens so pleased? Why had their Town Council, supportive of the new railway, been described in parliamentary cross-examination as 'the closest and most rotten corporation in Scotland'? And why had a North British Chairman spoken glowingly the previous year of the railway connecting 'the flourishing manufacturing towns along the line by Liddesdale', when there quite obviously were none?

Perhaps the 'Teries'—Hawick citizens—can be forgiven for so enthusiastically backing the wrong horse in terms of promoting a new

*The barren landscape south of Hawick is seen to advantage in this shot of a Class '26' diesel, then numbered D5308, powering an Edinburgh-Carlisle train southwards from Shankend on the climb to Whitrope on 5 June 1965.* (W. S. Sellar)

cross-Border railway. After all, they were not alone in wanting to see rails climbing southwards up the tight Slitrig valley to the watershed of Limekilnedge, into the former Reiver's territory of Liddesdale, and thence south to Carlisle. Most of the Border burghs (with the understandable exception of Langholm) were in favour of the route, but there seems little doubt that much inaccurate information was in circulation about the prospective main line.

In October 1856 Hawick Town Council received a report from a specially-constituted sub-committee which listed the apparent advantages of reaching Carlisle via Newcastleton rather than Langholm. It was shorter—37 miles from Hawick to Carlisle as opposed to 37 to Gretna—and involved 'no serious difficulties'. Within the month, there appeared to be some attempt to correct these errors—the distance was nearer 47 than 37, while the second part of the statement, which ignored the necessary surmounting of a 1,000-foot summit, does not bear serious examination. Unfortunately, the Town Council was by now divided along party lines, obscuring mere facts. Another incentive which attracted Hawick support was the prospect of coal from Plashetts, in Northumberland, rolling into Hawick to power the mills at 8s (40p) per ton. This of course was one of the potential (but ultimately illusory) benefits of having a line which connected with destinations other than just Carlisle, and was undoubtedly a cornerstone of the NBR policy on the vexed matter of choosing a southern route.

Minerals were of crucial importance in the decision-making process about the choice of route. The presiding Parliamentary commission was told that the Canonbie coalfield could generate 150,000 tons of coal for 110 years, while the Plashetts field on the Border Counties line could offer 400,000 tons for 260 years! The North British could argue that their line would service *both* fields, the Canonbie coal being transported along the Langholm branch southwards. Unfortunately Plashetts coal was to prove unsuitable for industrial use—something that might have been assessed by this time.

Possibly the North British felt it had no choice in the matter of route anyway; if the Caledonian was allowed by Parliament to 'occupy the ground' north of Langholm as appeared to be the case in the 1850s, then the Edinburgh company obviously saw itself as having no option to the Slitrig/Liddesdale route. Yet there is evidence that the Caledonian would not have been impossible to deal with had the NBR been able to countenance a Langholm route. In September 1857 a meeting was set up between representatives of the two companies, with the Duke of Buccleuch's agent, John Gibson, as arbiter. The Caledonian offered to operate the line (through the Mosspaul pass) for the first ten years only, but was unable to offer specific guarantees about through traffic after that time.

Certainly, the NBR could be forgiven for feeling uneasy about this lack of assurance, as well as the nature of the connection between the two companies planned for Hawick in the Caledonian prospectus of 1856. The company's main station would be at the Town Haugh, on the west side of the Teviot, approximately where the North British had been planning to site theirs ten years previously. There would be a link northwards, cited in the plans as a separate railway undertaking, to join the NBR at an end-on junction 'at a point within the Hawick branch' from Edinburgh. This would in fact have been immediately south of the existing covered Hawick station, making reversal necessary for a through Edinburgh-Carlisle service, unless the NBR prepared alternative or enlarged passenger facilites.

It was almost as if this extension was an afterthought, nothing more than a courtesy gesture to a neighbour company; it certainly did not seem to be projected as a link to create a new Anglo-Scottish route from Edinburgh to Carlisle (after all, the 'Caley' had one already), and a vital lifeline to make the Edinburgh-Hawick line financially viable.

Understandably, the September 1857 meeting between Caledonian and NBR representatives was doomed to failure. The North British could not shake off the suspicion that its rivals would have a strong vested interest in seeing the line south from Hawick operate at less than full efficiency to ensure that the Caledonian line via Carstairs would continue to cater for principal Edinburgh-Carlisle traffic. Also to be considered was its revenue from services between Aberdeen, Perth, Dundee and England which would also be affected if the North British obtained access to Carlisle, even if the latter company could not yet boast its own lines to all of these northern centres.

Only the historian can know that after 1865, with the NBR merging with the Edinburgh & Glasgow, the former company would then hold a formidable trump against its rival—part of the Caledonian's route from Carlisle to Aberdeen passed over the former Monklands Railway, now safely in the NBR fold. In other words, as the Scottish rail network spread over the country, numerous little interdependencies formed themselves between the companies, minimizing the likelihood of selfish and negative attitudes in principle, and of the Caledonian being obstructive at Hawick in particular. But how could the NBR Chairman, Richard Hodgson, have foreseen that? It was, after all, only ten years since the 'Caley' had been prepared to choke the southern end of the Glasgow & South Western main line at Gretna, as will be shown later.

On a more positive note, there is no doubt that the projected line south-eastwards from Hawick offered the North British a *double* route to the northern English cities on both east and west coasts. Obviously, Hodgson's friendship with Charlton, the Northumbrian businessman who was the moving spirit behind the Border Counties Railway, was a bond which was fundamental in promoting this hillier route south from Hawick and then establishing a junction in the hills to allow of a secondary route into England. At that time, the Newcastle & Carlisle was still outside the North Eastern Railway's ownership; if running powers could be obtained, this would bring the North British to the gates of Newcastle. (This, of course, did happen even after the NER had quickly secured its western flank by absorbing the N & C, but, as shown in the chapter on Lamberton, the North British had to pay an exorbitant price for entry into the Tyneside conurbation.)

The NBR's Board Minutes do not appear to disclose when the Company turned irretrievably from Teviotdale to Slitrig; perhaps the aborted meeting arranged by the Duke of Buccleuch's agent was the final nail in the coffin of a line through the Mosspaul pass. Whether the Caledonian was genuinely prepared to build one is now difficult to discern; certainly, Elliot believes that the announced plan of constructing only a single line northwards to Hawick suggests less than full-blooded determination to prepare a new route.

Sir James Graham, the North Cumberland landowner who was very much a friend of the Caledonian system—we shall see him in a later chapter as one of the first passengers on Gretna station platform waiting to join the inaugural northbound train—appeared disenchanted with the Company's blocking move. In 1858 he told the parliamentary committee that the Caledonian had 'occupied the country for five years, but did not make the line . . . being dissatisfied with the way the Caledonian Company acted before, I have given my support to the NB'. The Caledonian Board Minutes for the period referred to by Graham do not appear to contain any indication of the Directors' intentions in the matter, apart from a decision to discontinue what was described as the 'prosecution' of the Canonbie and Longtown branches in February 1853.

By November 1856, coincidentally exactly the same month that the Border Counties produced their impossibly ambitious survey plans for a line north to Belses, the Caledonian lodged its plans for a Carlisle-Hawick line with the local authorities. Surveyed by Messrs B. Hall Blyth and Thomas Bouch (the latter of Tay Bridge notoriety), the line was planned to leave the Caledonian main line at Mossband on the north bank of the Esk. The Border would have been crossed 5½ miles farther on, just before the Canonbie branch went off to the east. (Presumably this was a different undertaking from that abandoned 3½ years earlier.) North of Langholm the Mosspaul pass was attacked by 5 miles of 1 in 70, with an almost similar incline downhill on the other side of the summit. There were no tunnels planned, and strangely enough, no station shown at Hawick's Town Haugh. It would not have been as grand or expensive an undertaking as Miller's plan of 1846, but a workable one nevertheless.

Interestingly, there had been yet another, earlier, survey and plan made for a line over the Mosspaul watershed. This had been revealed in November 1852, ostensibly by an independent company, but with running powers exclusively leased to the North British. It thus predated the Caledonian's plans by some four years, despite the fact that the latter enjoyed parliamentary favour for building such a line. If there was a detailed Caledonian proposal at this time, it does not appear to have survived in the archives (the author would welcome any information to the contrary), although the 1856 survey would surely have been unnecessary had such a survey existed.

The ostensibly independent survey of 1852 was carried out by B. Hall Blyth (who was to carry out a repeat commission four years later) and Charles Jopp. This was remarkably similar to Miller's survey of six years before, although there would have been a fairly gruelling southern approach to Mosspaul of 6 miles at 1 in 70-90, complete with a 350-yard tunnel, with a shorter bore to the north of the summit. Junction with the Caledonian main line would have been effected east of the Esk in the Crookdyke area, presumably because the land immediately to the north belonged to the pro-Caledonian Sir James Graham.

This survey was doomed to gather dust in the files, but let there be no misunderstanding of the importance to the North British Board of pushing the Hawick line southwards. At the half-yearly meeting on 2 March 1858, the shareholders were told:

'Without extension to the South, it was obvious at first, and the experience of nine years has amply proved, that the resources of a large tract of country must remain undeveloped . . . and that nearly one half of the NBR System, instead of being remunerative to the Company, *must operate as a drawback on the profits of the remainder.*'

Here we see frankly stated the true uneconomic character of the Edinburgh-Hawick line, although the solution was hardly likely to alleviate the problem of non-viability. To make some 45 miles of unremunerative line viable, the company was going to construct another 45, through even more desolate country! It certainly proves what Elliot describes in his university thesis as 'the exaggerated belief in the developmental momentum created by railways'; Hodgson was quoted in September 1858 as talking about 'the flourishing manufacturing towns along the line by Liddesdale'. Did he mean after the railway opened? There were certainly none there beforehand, nor any afterwards.

Interestingly, only three years previously, a Mr Skynner of London, presumably a prominent stockholder, had successfully led a revolt against the southern-bent ambitions of the North British Board. When he declared that such an extension served only 'a few individual interests', the Minutes reveal that his was only one of many letters 'nearly, if not quite all, deprecating this Company subscribing to the proposed Hawick and Carlisle Railway'. A subsequent meeting, chaired by Hodgson, 'generally was adverse to the proposed subscription' and voted accordingly.

What we do know about this episode of confused manoeuvrings to bridge the 'railway gap' between Hawick and Carlisle is that there was consternation in Hawick when the Caledonian Railway Bill's Preamble was found 'proved' by the House of Commons in 1858. The town's senior magistrate, Bailie Oliver, was immediately asked to convene a special protest meeting—unfortunately, he was apparently the only member of the Council in favour of the Caledonian's route. He refused the request, but had no alternative to resignation. In parliamentary cross-examination, when questioned why the Town Council was in favour of the Liddesdale route, one witness dismissed them as 'the closest and most rotten Corporation in Scotland', citing the town's electorate as being 150 out of a population of 11-12,000. Ironically, it does appear that the Council was in step with popular opinion; Bailie Oliver was a minor martyr of the Railway Age.

The Lords found against the Caledonian scheme, and the whole rigmarole re-entered the parliamentary arena in the following session—for the fifth time, according to the *Railway Times*. It was unequivocally rooting for the North British, divining (probably correctly) that the Caledonian's scheme was nothing more than a blocking move. Less correct was the magazine's endorsement of Chairman Hodgson's remark that a southbound extension from Hawick via Riccarton 'will prove the most remunerative of any stock ever issued by the North British'.

In the subsequent cross-examination of witnesses before the parliamentary committee in 1859, both he and the magazine's contributor would have done well to listen to the opinion of Mark Turnbull, a Hawick miller:

'I would select Mosspaul as the best line. I don't think much of the Liddesdale line. The population is very small, and I send hardly anything there. There are only two coaches on the Langholm road; but I should think there would be about 100 carts going each day. There are no coaches and very few carts on the Liddesdale route.'

A breath of common sense in the smoke-filled rooms of Westminster? If so, it was doomed to go unheeded, even when no less a personage than the Duke of Buccleuch backed the Langholm route. His Grace reminded the committee of his consistency in supporting this route; he backed first the North British, then the Caledonian, depending on which company planned to put Langholm on a main line. Pointing out that each line currently proposed (including part of the Border Counties) occupied equally some 26 route miles on his land—a reminder of his power and influence in the south of Scotland—the Duke believed that the mineral potential of Liddesdale had been greatly exaggerated and basically consisted of enough lime for farm consumption on a localized basis.

Logic, and local knowledge, decreed that the future Waverley Route should proceed southwards via Langholm. The trouble was that the company empowered to build it was transparently not interested in doing so, giving a fair amount of moral impetus to the North British case to build via the alternative valley.

In retrospect, it seems tragic that some accommodation could not have been found to benefit both Caledonian and North British adversaries. The successive parliamentary committees of 1858-9 appear not to have discerned the dual nature of the question before them—should a railway line between Hawick and Carlisle be built via Langholm or via Limekilnedge, *and*, for this was basically a different matter entirely, should the North British be allowed to turn their Edinburgh-Hawick branch into a through Anglo-Scottish route or not? If the route via Langholm was the logical one, then surely a parliamentary assembly worth its salt should find accordingly, and both competing companies given the opportunity to show reason why each should be the obvious choice of company to build and operate it? If no decision could be reached, was the concept of a joint line out of the question? The Border Counties line could then remain as a private, localized initiative to offer a transport option for the North Tyne valley from the south, and its dreams of crossing the Border could have been allowed to disappear in the clouds of Knot-i-the-Gate.

To conclude this account of what is now history, John Miller's evidence should be briefly mentioned. This was the engineer, remember, who had produced by far the best plan for a Hawick-Carlisle line by either route, yet he told the Parliamentary committee in 1859:

'If I had known of the existence of the Liddesdale valley, I feel satisfied we should have carried it through Parliament in 1846 ... Since I have left engineering I have turned agriculturist ... and as an agriculturist, I entertain a high opinion of the advantages which the NB scheme will secure to the public'.

*Shankend Viaduct was proof that the old North British Railway saw their Border Union extension to Carlisle as worthy of considerable investment. Besides Shankend, there was another at Lynwood, as well as the ¾ mile of Whitrope tunnel. In this picture, a Class '26' diesel heads an Edinburgh-Carlisle train southwards on 2 December 1961. (W. S. Sellar)*

It was a sad contribution from a deservedly eminent contributor to Scotland's railway history. Was Miller really unaware of the alternative potential route 13 years earlier? And did his new career blind him to the engineering problems Limekilnedge would pose?

Royal assent for the Border Union Railway, to connect Hawick with the Port Carlisle Railway terminus in Carlisle via Riccarton, was received in the summer of 1859, with nine construction contracts being given out by the early autumn, and construction beginning on 7 October. The contracted areas were Hawick, Whitrope, Riccarton, Hermitage, Castleton, Penton, Netherby, Carlisle and Gretna. The main line would be 44 miles 115 yards long, costing a predicted £339,000. It would be double track throughout except for its central section between the BCR and Langholm branch junctions (ie Riccarton-Riddings). Eight stations were planned for the main line—Shankend, Riccarton, Newcastleton, Penton, Langholm Road (near Scotch Dyke), Longtown, Parkhouse, and at one other, unnamed site (probably Barnes, later renamed Stobs). The 6-mile Langholm branch was costed at just under £50,000 and would have two stations, at Canonbie and Limefoot, but as we shall see in the next chapter, would be delayed—as a 'punishment' to the townspeople!

Use would be made of the Port Carlisle line's terminus at Carlisle, until entry to Citadel was arranged. A 4-mile toll for the 1¼ miles thence to Citadel would be exacted by the Caledonian; a fair rate, thought the *Railway Times*, given the expensive nature of urban rail construction. The NBR was absorbing the Port Carlisle and Silloth lines, both of their owning companies investing in the Border Union.

*       *       *

And so began the construction of the last main line to cross the Border. As if to punish the North British for its choice of route, fate decreed that the winters of 1859 and 1860 were the worst for many years. The NBR Minutes contain periodic reports of committees of inspection despatched to the Cheviots to report on progress, and much can be read between the lines of their accounts.

The contractor responsible for the Hawick section, involving the bridging of the Teviot in Hawick itself and of the Slitrig at Lynnwood, caused concern from the outset. The latter viaduct had to be strengthened before completion, while the foundations of the former construction proved to be inadequate. By the beginning of 1862, a visiting committee of Directors expressed dismay at the slow progress of the work there—which did not share the problems of remoteness met with by contractors farther south—and urged Thompson, the contractor, to take on extra men. The Directors were not able to do this personally as they found that Thompson 'evaded' them on their visit.

Whitrope tunnel was the major construction challenge. Although not incomparably long at 1,206 yards, the isolated location of the works added to the arduous nature of its construction. In 1861 NBR Director Edmund Bowman was shocked to find navvies outside the tunnel area 'on holiday'; he was informed that the men could not work with their coats on, and were soon soaked through without them. This was outdoors in fairly typical weather; inside the bore, conditions were no better.

'Ritson is disheartened and will stop unless he is helped.' The Whitrope contractor had to be given suitable financial encouragement to press on with this marathon earthwork, which employed hundreds of workmen at ten faces underground. It was estimated that more than 400 gallons of water were pouring into the tunnel each minute, and a troublesome watercourse had to be redirected.

Working on such a project in the middle of the bleak Cheviot hills, with no sizeable village for miles, hardly bears thinking about. Small wonder that the navvies sought their pleasure at the 'Turf Hotel' at Shankend, a hostelry that proved (perhaps mercifully) to be as temporary as the Whitrope tunnel is permanent. The latter construction is still to be seen; on the author's last visit, standing at the southern mouth of this dank, forbidding bore, my breath turned to steam in the cold air from under the Border moors, this on a hot August day.

The 1862 visiting committee, which was so concerned with the incomplete state of the Hawick works, was well pleased with progress at Whitrope. No delay resulted from this construction, and the long-awaited,much-debated line between Hawick and Carlisle opened at last on 1 July 1862. (The Carlisle-Riddings section appears to have been operating since November 1861, along with the Langholm branch as far as Canonbie.) The section from Riccarton to Riddings comprised single track, despite a decision in March 1861 that it should be doubled. In fact, the Riddings-Kershopefoot stretch was taken in hand for doubling straight away after opening; a strange decision, as it may well have appeared obvious that a single line was perfectly adequate for traffic at that time.

'Traffic on the new mileage is increasing at a satisfactory rate: arrangements for through booking and interchange of rolling stock with foreign companies are either adjusted or in negotiation; new sources of Local Traffic are being discussed.'

This was the somewhat over-optimistic report given to the stockholders at the NBR's half-yearly meeting in September 1862. It would be obvious to even the least well-informed investor in railways that the North British could expect no traffic at Carlisle from the LNWR main line from the south. Nor was there any profusion of contacts with the GSWR at Gretna, the NBR Board noting the previous year—rather late in the day, one might think—that the Glasgow Company was contractually committed to the Caledonian as far as Portpatrick traffic was concerned, so prospects for Edinburgh-Belfast traffic via the new Waverley Route (as it was called from its opening in 1862) were no more real than that of passengers from Euston or the great cities of Lancashire joining the North British trains at Carlisle.

'The Directors regret that the increase in traffic receipts, although considerable in amount, has not kept pace with the increased mileage of Railway opened, and Trains run.'

This was the more realistic message from the Board at the next half-yearly meeting, a general downturn in business and shipping being held to blame. The LNWR's refusal to allow Midland-North British traffic over the Lancaster and Carlisle line between Ingleton and Carlisle was highlighted as a factor in the NBR's disappointing performance, and the Directors complained that they were being excluded from the existing 'English and Scotch Traffic Agreement'. Hardly an unpredictable turn of events, and one where the Edinburgh Company's attitude seems irrational; why did the NBR Directors expect a free exchange of traffic with the companies south of Carlisle when they had not expected any such facility at Hawick if the Caledonian had occupied the line south of there? When the option of a joint route had been proposed by the Duke of Buccleuch's agent in 1857, the North British suspected the same element of obstructiveness from the Caledonian that it seemed surprised to find from that company's southern ally.

One source of local traffic being discussed was a cattle market

*An idea of the amount of freight channelled on to the Waverley Route can be gleaned from this picture looking north from Riccarton on 16 July 1963. 'A1' 'Pacific' No 60118* Archibald Sturrock, *carrying a Leeds shedplate, arrives on a Millerhill-Carlisle freight, her fireman running ahead to the station buildings. An Edinburgh-based 'V2', No 60957, waits to head a Millerhill freight northwards on the down line.* (W. S. Sellar)

which the NBR, in September 1862, suggested that the Hawick Town Council should help set up in the town, to be held weekly or fortnightly. It was close to the station, and rail-connected, moving as many as 78,000 sheep in 1935. By 1954 only 20 per cent of this moved by rail, and by 1963 the traffic had almost completely ended, indicating its importance to the Waverley Route's revenue statistics, and reflecting credit on the NBR's initiative in generating traffic.

In 1865 Captain O'Brien, General Manager of the North Eastern Railway, informed a parliamentary committee that over the years 1861-3, Anglo-Scottish freight traffic on the East Coast Main Line had declined from 4,045 tons in the former years to only 624 tons in the latter. These figures represent a remarkable decline coinciding with the opening of the Edinburgh-Hawick-Carlisle line as a through route for freight, as opposed to passenger, traffic.

With two summits of around 900-1,000 feet, and a serpentine succession of curves throughout, the 98 miles of the Waverley route was arguably the most operationally difficult main line in Britain. Although approximately 2 miles shorter than the Caledonian's line via Carstairs, there was never any prospect or expectation of the NBR vying with its western rival in terms of speed between Edinburgh and Carlisle; indeed, there was no point in attempting to do so, since the new line carried no passenger traffic to and from London until 1876.

In that year the Midland completed its magnificent Settle and Carlisle line, in a manner which must have made North British enginemen view their new English colleagues with envy. While mounting an even higher summit (Aisgill, at approximately 1,150 feet), the Midland had engineered its gradients at a steady 1 in 100, but eliminated troublesome curves with a considerable number of earthworks. As a result, 2 hr 20 min became a reasonably attainable journey time for the 113 miles from Leeds, while in the northern direction 'even time' descents from the heights of north Yorkshire to the portals of Carlisle's Citadel station were commonplace. Indeed, Britain's first officially-timed 'ninety' was recorded by the first Midland Compound on this route, so, hills or not, it was undoubtedly a line fit for expresses.

Yet the Waverley line saw some stirring locomotive work from the time it first carried London expresses. In preparation for its opening as a through route in 1876 (in the 14 years since its opening to Carlisle in 1862 only light cross-country passenger traffic was carried), Dugald Drummond designed the '476' Class of 4-4-0s to take over from the weaker Wheatley '420' 4-4-0s. These new engines, soon to be referred to as the 'Abbotsford' Class, after Sir Walter Scott's famous home on the Tweed near Melrose, took their place in the mainstream of the NBR's 4-4-0 production almost until Grouping in 1923. They were among the largest of British express engines at the time of their introduction, and according to the RCTS history of the class 'were not significantly exceeded in size and power by any British passenger engine for almost twenty years'. These robust units were soon attaining highly respectable 140-minute non-stop timings on the line—much the same timing achieved by the Midland south of Carlisle on a line 15 miles longer, but with only one major summit.

While NBR enginemen won the respect of their peers in the Carlisle railway community for the invariably high standard of passenger train operation over the line, there was never any question of Midland-North British Anglo-Scottish expresses challenging their counterparts on the East and West Coasts in terms of speeds, and the Railway Races of 1888 and 1895 passed them by (ironically so, in the case of the second of these races when the target was Aberdeen, as the Midland had put even more capital into the financing of the Forth Bridge, which made the 1895 Race possible, than did either of the English East Coast Companies).

With speed comparisons out of the question, the Midland and NBR concentrated more on palatial-like comfort for first class passengers, third class seats available on every train, and milking the literary interests of the Border country ('The land of Scott') for publicity value.

However, in 1901 an event occurred which pushed the Waverley Route into the limelight as an Anglo-Scottish trunk line. A third 'Race to the North' broke out!

Reorganization within the Midland Railway saw Lord Farrer, one of its Directors, charged with the task of improving long-distance express services, and he decided that St Pancras's services to and from Edinburgh and Glasgow should not stop more than four times south of the Border, including Carlisle. The English Company lost no time in urging its Scottish allies to improve their part of the service, and meetings were held at St Pancras and York.

The proposal to accelerate trains between Carlisle and Edinburgh came at an awkward time for the NBR, which was still in the throes of its chronic dispute with the North Eastern, discussed in previous chapters. Truth to tell, relations between Edinburgh and St Pancras were sometimes not much better; as mentioned, the Midland on at least one occasion despatched an employee to Waverley Station to ensure that the NBR was not displaying too many advertisements for the East Coast route to London! As related in this author's book on the subject of the 1901 episode (see Bibliography), both Midland and North Eastern Companies suspected that it would be only natural for the Edinburgh-based Company to play one of its English allies off against the other. In fact, there is little or no evidence of this happening, possibly because the North British had quite enough to occupy its attention within Scotland where it was in constant competition with the Caledonian, and it appears to have dealt honestly, if at times stolidly and unimaginatively, with its counterparts south of the Tweed and Solway.

Urged to accelerate its Waverley Route expresses, the NBR Directors agreed to do so in their first meeting with the Midland, leaving the details to be worked out by the Company's officers at the second conference. The Minutes of this meeting show that the Edinburgh Company agreed to cut 5 minutes from the Waverley Route timing, bringing it down to 135 minutes for the 98 miles non-stop. This meant that the 09.30 ex-St Pancras was now due into Edinburgh only 10 minutes before the down East Coast 'Flying Scotsman', giving Portobello East Junction, 3 miles east of Waverley, the character of a 'finishing-post', like Kinnaber Junction in the 1895 contest. The new timetable was due to be introduced on Monday 1 July 1901.

A total of 135 minutes was the fastest ever timing scheduled for the line until then; perhaps it can be put into perspective by recalling that in 1954 the crack 'Elizabethan' express, with an 'A4' in good nick, was diverted northwards over the Waverley Route, taking all of 162 minutes over the 98 miles, while on one of the last occasions the author travelled southbound on the line the Class '46' diesel took 166 minutes, admittedly with five stops. Of course, running non-stop created its own problems for the NBR crews. By 1901 the '729' Class of 4-4-0s designed by Matthew Holmes had taken over from their Drummond predecessors, but the new Holmes engines had only 3,500-gallon capacity tenders. With no possibility of water-trough replenishment on the move—there was scarcely a straight stretch long enough!—the crews could never relax their vigilance over water consumption. How the 'Abbotsfords' had previously managed to run non-stop with 1,000 gallons *less* is a matter for conjecture and marvel.

Having set the scene, only a summary of the NBR's involvement in the comparatively little-known 1901 race can be included here. The North Eastern made a daily practice of leaving Newcastle punctually with the 'Scotsman' and then gaining unprecedented amounts of time on the way north, particularly on their own tracks south of Berwick. North of the Border, the NBR signalmen often seemed somewhat slower than their English counterparts in setting the signals! The West Coast made a meteoric appearance in the race on the Friday of that week, chopping 35 minutes from their schedule into Edinburgh's Princes Street terminus and leaving even the North Eastern gasping for breath.

How could the North British compete against these aces? With no tradition for fast running, with a main line originally intended as a horse-drawn waggonway for part of its length, the NBR nevertheless prepared to enter the 1901 race.

The opening day of racing produced a superb northbound run on the Waverley Route, timed in detail by the railway correspondent of *The Scotsman* newspaper, believed to have been Norman McDonald. It is worth examining this run in detail, not only because it represents one of the fastest ever traverses of the Waverley Route by a revenue-earning passenger train but also because it symbolizes the unfailingly high standard of the locomotive work on the line from the first year when Anglo-Scottish expresses started passing through Kershopefoot. In 1877 the brand-new 'Abbotsfords' had prompted the author Professor Foxwell to talk of 'the very best express running in the world over such hills', while William Ackworth had compared Waverley Route performance favourably with the best of European rail operating. All the more reason to celebrate the NBR's entry into the 1901 Race on Monday 1 July.

Despite good running by a Johnson 'single' south of Leicester, the Midland had brought the 9.30 some 6½ minutes late into Carlisle. Here brake systems had to be changed—the Midland used the vacuum brake, the NBR the Westinghouse—and more time was lost. Indeed, in the seven days of racing that made up the 1901 episode, the Carlisle changeover was not completed once in the 5 minutes allowed. So, 9 minutes late, North British 4-4-0 No 738 set out northwards with a load of five coaches, grossing 150 tons, in her bid to beat the North Eastern to Scotland's capital.

'Excellent work at once began,' reported *The Scotsman*. Longtown (9½ miles) was passed in only 12¼ minutes, and Riddings (14¼ miles) taken at 62 mph in 17½ minutes. The next 18¼ miles to Riccarton were nearly all uphill, the train passing into Scotland at Kershopefoot, and this stretch understandably occupied 27½ minutes. Probably the driver was reluctant to tire his fireman with two-thirds of the run still to go, while the spectre of running short of water was ever present. Indeed, within three days a Midland train taking part in the Race ran 'dry' at Blea Moor, on the Settle and Carlisle line. Racing against the North Eastern, an unscheduled stop meant inevitable defeat.

After topping Whitrope, No 738 dived into the tunnel, her immediate climb over. Not surprisingly, speed was not allowed to exceed 61 mph on the sharp bends downhill to Hawick, 45½ miles being accomplished in 62 minutes. On the comparatively easier section to Galashiels, mile-a-minute rates were recorded at St Boswells and Melrose, these 19¼ miles being run in 21½ minutes. 'Here it was realized,' reported McDonald, 'that the train was making a very fine run, and hopes rose that Edinburgh might be reached in time.' Galashiels was passed slowly and the climb to Falahill began.

Up the valley of the Gala Water went the 09.30, her progress being recorded and timed by both McDonald and the Rev W. J. Scott, veterans of the 1895 conflict. (Incidentally, Scott gave the locomotive's number as 733, although McDonald's seems likely to be the more accurate observation, as he had accompanied the engine up from Edinburgh that morning.) Falahill summit, some 900 feet above sea level, was attained in 105 minutes from Carlisle, and her driver then gave 738 her head as she stormed towards Edinburgh. Despite the curves and mining slacks, a mile a minute was averaged downhill towards Portobello. Would she beat the North Eastern into Waverley? Was a punctual arrival possible after a 9 minute late start from Carlisle over Britain's worst main line?

Niddrie North signals were 'off—she was cleared through Portobello East! No 738 brought her train on to the East Coast Main Line with no sign of a train signalled from the Berwick direction. After a journey of more than 400 miles, the 09.30 was on the last lap of the race.

Who won the 1901 outburst of racing? The interested reader is directed to this author's book already mentioned. Suffice to say that 738's efforts were not sufficient to beat a rival which had been held for 7 minutes (purposely, one suspects) at Berwick but which still beat the North British by a margin of 4 minutes. Matters got steadily worse as the week went on, with the NBR being pushed into third place when the London & North Western and Caledonian companies made their dramatic entry into the contest on Friday 5 July. Little wonder perhaps that such respected writers as O. S. Nock and the late Cecil J. Allen have dismissed the NBR's participation in the Race as being less than noteworthy. Allen was particularly scathing in his 1964 publication *The North Eastern Railway*, his opinion appearing to be at some variance with the contemporary—and by no means exclusively Scottish—newspapers reporting the episode. Mr Nock goes further, dismissing any idea of the North British coming sufficiently close to its apparently superior North Eastern rival as to pose a problem for the signalman at Portobello East—who should be given precedence over the remaining 3½ miles into Waverley? Yet the records show that precisely this *did* happen on the last day of the Race, Monday 8 July!

At about six o'clock on that second Monday of the 1901 Race, the NBR signalman at Portobello East Junction almost certainly learned that two express trains were approaching his box simultaneously. One was the 'Flying Scotsman' speeding along the East Coast Main Line in the direction of Joppa, the last box before the junction, the other was the NB's own train, the 9.30 ex-St Pancras. Which one would he give precedence to, for the final 3½ miles to Waverley? There was never any doubt on that score.

For once the Midland had excelled itself, a Class '2606' 4-4-0 bringing the 'racer' into Carlisle more than 5 minutes early. The North British waited for time before departing and the schedule was strictly kept. Portobello East was passed at just on 6 o'clock—there was no nonsense about the signalman making a sporting gesture to the North Eastern rival—and Waverley was reached punctually. This author estimates that the NER train was probably in sight as its Scottish rival went through; there was more than a hint of favouritism, as implied in the newspaper reports of the time. Before the NBR is accused of unsportsmanlike behaviour, it should be explained that the NER train was officially scheduled to arrive later than the NBR one anyway, and that the NER's unofficial timing was in breach of the agreement on Anglo-Scottish train timings that both Companies had signed only five years earlier.

Nevertheless, the North British had succeeded in beating its East Coast rival, and, in view of the lack of subsequent competition, it seems that pride was considered satisfied on all sides. The North British had shown that, difficult route or not, it could operate express passenger services to the highest standard.

The imagination has to really strain nowadays to imagine a Holmes '729' 4-4-0 hurrying its northbound train over the level crossing at Kershopefoot station, across the nearby Border bridge, and then up the steepening foothills of Liddesdale. The erstwhile Waverley Route

*Class 'A3' 'Pacifics' took over the major workings on the Waverley Route from the Reid 'Atlantics' from 1929, those based at Carlisle (Canal) being a well-known sight for Border travellers. This is one of their Scottish-based sisters, No 60098 Spion Kop, approaching Riddings Junction with a northbound relief express on 28 July 1962. (Douglas Hume)*

*Closure of the Waverley Route was still 4½ years away when this picture of Kershopefoot was taken looking south on a day late in May 1964. Ivatt '4MT' No 43028 heads tender-first towards Hawick with a pick-up freight from Carlisle.* (Douglas Hume)

at this location could be any farm-track or Forestry Commission access path. One has to pinch oneself to remember that this was once a railway line which O. S. Nock described as 'no place for weak or ailing engines'.

\*     \*     \*

After the nationalization of the railways in 1948, it was inevitable that the need for two lines between Edinburgh and Carlisle would be questioned. The former Caledonian route could effectively be (and still is) operated as a branch off the Carlisle-Glasgow main line, and in any event offered a much faster route between the Border city and the Scottish capital. The Waverley Route's main function was to provide a direct link between the textile producing areas of the Borders and West Yorkshire, although such traffic may hardly have been sufficient to sustain its viability. There was also considerable traffic on the central Galashiels-Hawick section. The author well remembers making a journey on the southbound 'Waverley' one Saturday in September 1968; the train was well filled for most of the journey, but between Galashiels and Hawick it was 'standing room only'! But even this revenue could scarcely compensate for the lack of receipts generated from the empty miles of Liddesdale moorland between there and Carlisle.

The Waverley Route's closure debate in the second half of the 1960s generated, in the words of H. P. White, 'more heat than light'. Commenting on the Borders' lack of a powerful political presence in London comparable to the Highland and Welsh lobbies (a fair comment; the area had not long previously elected a comparatively inexperienced Liberal MP called David Steel), the Waverley line was up against it from the start.

Not that the Borderers let their railway go without a struggle.

Feelings were running high on the final day of services, Sunday 5 January 1969. An excursion specially arranged by BR's Scottish Region the previous day was perhaps not a diplomatic act by the railway managers, although it was undoubtedly a profitable one. Some 340 adults and 70 children paid a total of nearly £850 for the privilege of travelling over the doomed line in nine coaches behind Class '47' No 1974. The journey out from Edinburgh was delayed by a bomb hoax, which caused police officers to join, and inspect, the train at Millerhill, while at Hawick a coffin was on display for despatch to London by a later train.

The last passenger working to traverse the entire route in the northbound direction was another enthusiasts' special, this time originating from Yorkshire, and hauled by Class '55' 'Deltic' No D9007 *Pinza*.

The last southbound working—the 21.55 ex-Edinburgh (Waverley)—was not destined to make an untroubled journey, and figured in one of the most extraordinary delays ever inflicted on a British train since the Great Train Robbery. Given the honour of signing off on the route was D60 *Lytham St Annes*, displaying a 1M82 headcode. The diesel was the successor of No 738 which had run so valiantly against the racers of the East and West Coasts, and had been succeeded in the fullness of time by hard-working Reid 'Atlantics' and Gresley 'Pacifics', whose combined domination of express workings on the line totalled some 55 years. Seen off from Galashiels by the local Provost, she had a less formal farewell from Hawick, where it was adjudged necessary to send a pilot locomotive—a Class '17' diesel—ahead to ensure that the line would be clear.

It was already known that there might be trouble at Newcastleton (the local TV station had been invited to send their cameras), and sure enough, the express arrived there to find the crossing gates closed and locked against it, with local citizens pushing a BR Landrover on to the track to further make their point. David Steel MP, a passenger on the train, appealed to his constituents to disperse, which they declined to do, the local minister, the Rev Brydon Mabon, being particularly angered by the closure. Thirty policemen were ferried in from Hawick by road in six vehicles, and the minister was led away, although not charged.

The express was already 30 minutes late on arrival at Newcastleton, where its delay was to stretch to an additional 80 minutes before the track was cleared and the final train from the Central Scottish Borders departed into the darkness. Unfortunately, the TV cameras had not turned up to record the fracas, which might have been useful visual evidence of how the public felt about losing their railway—after all, the 'hold-up' of a main-line express is not exactly a daily event.

Even the opportunity of a subsidy proviso in the recent 1968 Transport Act would not act as a life-saver. As White comments aptly in his book *Forgotten Railways*,

'the protestors probably made a tactical error in concentrating on trying to keep the whole line open, for by doing so they drew attention [away] from the less costly alternative of a 52¾ mile, DMU-operated, "basic" railway between Edinburgh and Hawick.'

It appears that there would have been a perfectly valid case for preserving the North British Railway's original Hawick branch, perhaps reduced to single track, and probably with passing loops at, say, Falahill and Galashiels. White argues that, assuming no economies—and there was plenty of scope for those—a subsidy of 4½p would be needed for every 1½p taken in fares on the Hawick section, yet other lines were receiving subsidies of up to 5p per fare. In contrast, the whole Waverley line would have required an astronomical 100p subsidy per fare. Certainly, figures published at the time by the Scottish Railway Development Association suggested that the existing £50,000 annual revenue on the line north of Hawick could be trebled by closing certain of the more unremunerative stations and allowing more local management initiatives to encourage traffic. Claiming that 5,000 people used the trains every week, the Association reckoned that the existing annual deficit of £300,000 could be slashed by improved turnover plus a reasonable grant.

One newspaper specifically commented that Mr Steel's journey to London on the last, and much delayed, 21.55 southwards down the Waverley Route, was undertaken on a mission to urge the Transport Minister to retain at least the line north of Hawick.

Unfortunately, local politics, or perhaps even simple naivety, may have prevented a more positive closure campaign being conducted.

*A pick-up freight headed by '4MT' No 43049 crosses from Scotland to England at Kershopefoot in April 1967 with goods vehicles from both Langholm and Newcastleton for Carlisle. (R. B. McCartney)*

There certainly was a crying need for economies in working practices, to say nothing of an imaginative attempt to attract tourists. If the preservation campaign was ill-conceived in attempting to retain the line as a through route, perhaps this was because there was some interest among English rail enthusiasts in preserving the line *in toto*; its return to its pre-1862 status as an Edinburgh-Hawick branch would obviously have alienated such English interest. Even this Edinburgh-Hawick reduced option would have demanded a fairly vigorous campaign from local authorities and individuals. But the creation of a Borders Region was still some four years in the future, so the protest from the area's local authorities (mostly quite small in population terms) was necessarily dissipated making doubly difficult a concerted area campaign against closure.

But there is certainly no need to assume, as some road-minded authorities have, that the central Borders area does not miss the railway. Some ten years after closure, the Policy Studies Institute (see Bibliography under Hillman, Meyer) found that hardship was still caused in the Newtown St Boswells area by the loss of rail services. The replacement bus services often followed a different route network, producing huge anomalies in the service pattern. The inhabitants of Newtown St Boswells now had four bus services *per week* to Hawick in place of 44 trains. Replacement road services between Galashiels and Hawick went, and still go, via Ashkirk and Selkirk, instead of following the railway's route, but it can scarcely be argued that a reasonable substitute service is available. Travelling times were also vastly inferior—Newtown to Hawick in 55-68 minutes by bus instead of 13-19 by rail. The Edinburgh-Hawick bus journey in 1970 was 3¼ hours instead of the train's 78 minutes, although this funereal pace has since been accelerated, following road improvements.

The Policy Studies Institute study of the Waverley Route closure found that Hawick, not surprisingly, lost much shop custom from the areas surrounding wayside stations to its rival neighbouring town of Galashiels, making more tragic (from Hawick's point of view) the misdirected aim of the preservation effort, such as it was.

The author well remembers that, barely a year after closure of the Waverley Route, the Scottish bus services, so lauded as a suitable replacement for the train, went on strike. For quite some time, Hawick's *only* public means of contact with the outside world was an occasional Carlisle-based bus service through Langholm. To travel directly by public transport to the Scottish capital, 50 miles away, was impossible. Shortly afterwards, the road transport lobby published a full-page advertisement in *The Times* extolling the benefits of road over rail and citing Hawick in particular as an example of a community 'benefiting' from being 40 miles from a railhead. One wonders if the 'Teries' (among whom the author was living in 1970) had been asked their opinion on the matter. Certainly there would be little chance of them journeying to London to protest!

# RIDDINGS BRIDGE

## Langholm Branch

This viaduct was not only the fifth Border crossing from east to west, but also the entry point for trains from the Waverley route on to the attractive Langholm branch. Langholm is the only sizeable town between Carlisle and Hawick in the central Borders, making it a logical stopping-place on a route between these centres via the Mosspaul pass. However, as we have seen in the previous chapter, history decreed that the North British—probably the only company genuinely wishing to connect Hawick and Carlisle—chose, or were forced to accept, the alternative Liddesdale route.

Obviously, this chapter will not go over that ground again. In addition, there is a definitive history of the Langholm branch at present being written (see Bibliography), so the account here will be necessarily brief. Suffice to say that Langholm received a branch from the NBR's uneconomic main line which climbed over the barren hills to the east of the town.

*    *    *

'Properly speaking ... Langholm is Caledonian ground'—Lord Portman, 1858.

'The North British, instead of encouraging the Caledonian to commit the suicidal act of constructing the Railway between Hawick and Carlisle, and so ... [ensure] the bankruptcy of a rival, [instead] opposed the deed, and after 2 or 3 years fighting, sewed the weapon for their own destruction.'
*A Losing N.B. Shareholder.* (1870 pamphlet)

'Suicidal', 'bankruptcy', 'destruction'. Anyone viewing the present-day remains of Riddings Viaduct cannot fail to be astonished that this quiet byway ever generated such passion. Today's railway historian can only look back at the railways of the central Borders through a glass dark with economic failure and rural depopulation. The coming

*Class '26' No D5304 begins its climb towards Whitrope with the 09.20 Carlisle-Edinburgh (Waverley) semi-fast on 25 May 1964. The Langholm branch on Riddings viaduct in the background still had another three weeks of passenger services ahead at this time. (Douglas Hume)*

of the railway in the nineteenth century was supposed to create a new prosperity for the area, although there is every indication that the Companies, and particularly the NBR, also saw the Borders as an area to be transected on the way to Newcastle, to Carlisle, to the Irish Sea, to Ireland.

We have already seen that the North British vacillated in its attitude to extending its Hawick branch farther south in the 1840s. At one time it was prepared to permit the Glasgow, Dumfries & Carlisle to operate such a line; within a year it was planning one itself. Both lines would have been built through Langholm, a town on which the Caledonian also had its beady eye. Obviously, whichever company built into Langholm would dominate the route northwards to the Mosspaul pass and thence into the central Borders.

Even as the Caledonian Directors were celebrating their triumph at Westminster in 1845 (of which more will be said in the next chapter) their thoughts certainly encompassed the need to build a branch to Langholm. Two major Border landowners who were also among the company's strongest supporters early in that year, Sir James Graham and the Duke of Buccleuch, reserved the right to support a line towards Carlisle from Hawick. They were certainly talking to the North British at this time; presumably both felt that a line southwards from Hawick was no more than logical.

In November 1845 the Caledonian Directors were told that a Langholm branch 'would have a considerable traffic in minerals' (its strategic value was not mentioned), and the following month plans for a branch to Canonbie were sent for the approval of the Duke of Buccleuch, owner of the coal-mines there. By the following April

*The viaduct in 1988, overgrown with vegetation. Both views are looking southwards.* (Author)

these two ideas were being sensibly combined as a Langholm branch with a Canonbie connection.

At this time, not a yard of track yet crossed the Border, yet both the later protagonists of Scottish railway history—the North British and Caledonian—viewed the small Border town of Langholm as a major objective for their future lines. That the 'Muckle toon', as it is colloquially called, had finally to make do with a branch from the North British, and not from the Caledonian, which might have given it some connection with other Dumfriesshire towns, is a matter for some surprise. The above quotation from Lord Portman, who chaired the parliamentary committee considering the choice of route, underlines this.

\*   \*   \*

One day in May 1858 the *Carlisle Patriot* reported that many of the townspeople of Langholm had begun walking along the public road to the English border, to catch first glimpse of a horse-drawn gig coming from the Carlisle direction. They had been promised that the horse would be beribboned in the colours of the company which had been given House of Commons approval to construct a line between Carlisle and Hawick by either Langholm or Liddesdale. It was a vital decision for the people of the industrious Border town; if the Caledonian company won the right to proceed with a line to Hawick, they would have main-line trains to north and south; if the North British were triumphant, they would be on the end of a branch line.

At last the messenger came in sight. The horse wore red ribbons. The townspeople went wild; for some reason not stated by the newspaper, this was the colour of the Teviotdale (Caledonian) lobby. 'Never was there so much joyous excitement in the town, within the memory of man.' A brass band lurking near the town square immediately struck up, bells were rung and 20 shots fired from the town cannon. Speeches from local worthies were drowned in cheers, the Duke of Buccleuch in particular being the toast of the town. Even some Hawick people celebrated, it appeared, although not all of them, while the news was received hard farther north in the North British Boardroom. Langholm's delight was, unfortunately, not just premature, but mistaken.

The proposal to build a Caledonian line to Hawick via Langholm northwards from a junction on the Carlisle-Gretna section of the West Coast Main Line was passed by the House of Commons that year, but thrown out in the Lords. The whole process had to be gone through again the following year, at the end of which time, as we have seen in the last chapter, the North British received the right to build *their* main line between Hawick and Carlisle—via Whitrope. There is no need to labour the point that this was a bad decision for all concerned; rather, its impact on the town of Langholm should now be examined in more detail.

Under the legislation of 1859, Langholm was to receive a 6-mile branch from the south, but there was a catch:

'Your directors (have) availed themselves of the opportunity to introduce a clause postponing the formation of their Langholm branch until twelve months after the opening of the main line to Carlisle for traffic.'

This is how NBR stockholders heard, on 6 September 1859, of the future rail provision to Langholm. Any suspicion that the citizens of that town were being 'punished' for their opposition to the company's

*Riddings Junction, only yards from the Anglo-Scottish border, but with the Waverley Route still in England despite Carlisle being nearly 15 miles away. Looking south, this view shows the 06.40 Edinburgh-Carlisle, the successor to the traditional 'Parliamentary', leaving behind Class '26' No D5303, having generated very little business for 'J39' No 64895 on the 10.06 for Langholm. (Douglas Hume)*

*Langholme-bound, Ivatt '4MT' No 43000 crosses the Liddel on the Riddings viaduct shortly after leaving the junction on the Waverley Route on 6 April 1963. (Douglas Hume)*

plans may well be underlined by a comment in a contemporary copy of the *Railway Times*:

'The Langholm branch . . . may be proceeded with immediately, should the local promoters furnish the capital they were prepared to provide for the competing but rejected scheme.'

Hardly a fair comment, given that the alternative scheme was for a main line which might well have provided through transport, without change of train, between Langholm and Edinburgh or Euston.

So Langholm eventually got its railway. Construction began between Langholm Junction (later Riddings) on the Waverley Route and Canonbie soon after Parliamentary approval was received, and the line was ready for traffic between these points as early as the autumn of 1861. Obviously the NBR looked on Canonbie coal as a valuable freight commodity, and it needed all the revenue it could get from its new Waverley Route investment, which was to be denied traffic from London and the English Midlands until well into the next decade. A contract for the completion of the branch from Canonbie to the branch terminus was given out to a Dunfermline company for £38,200 in the autumn of 1862.

Public services into Langholm itself began on Monday 18 April 1864, nearly a year longer than the delay promised by the NBR, avenging itself on the Langholm-based supporters of the Caledonian scheme. In fact, the long-awaited introduction of passenger trains into Langholm was a shambles. Within only a few days of opening, one arch of the Byreburn viaduct collapsed, and the rest of the structure threatened to follow it. The NBR's consulting engineer blamed the recent wet weather preventing the structure 'settling' properly, and felt that the brickwork was insufficiently bonded. The contractor saw it differently, however, pointing out that the NBR's decision in January 1863 to reopen a coal-mining shaft directly under the viaduct's piers was hardly conducive to its future safety! Although an arbiter had to be called in to settle the question of culpability, it seems incredible that the company thought it could get away with blaming the builder in these circumstances, and money eventually had to be handed over to another contractor for repairs.

Unfortunately for the citizens of the Border town, their coach service had already been withdrawn, and for some time they lacked any public transport to and from the outside world. Not surprisingly, the Board of Trade was asked to look into the matter of the new branch line, but it seems that trains did not run again on the branch until October.

For the next hundred years Langholm was served reasonably well by passenger trains, many of them running through to Carlisle, others connecting with trains on the Waverley Route at Riddings, where the down platform was an island whose western edge served the branch. The 1910 timetable shows seven passenger workings each way, taking around 20 minutes for the journey. There was one through evening working each way between the branch terminus and Carlisle. By 1952 this had been increased to three in the up direction (two on Saturdays) plus three to Riddings only. There were five down passenger services, only one of them advertised to run from Carlisle.

No effort appears to have been made to introduce services to Dumfries in conjunction with the Glasgow & South Western at Gretna; as discussed in the next chapter, there was a need for Langholm citizens to carry out 'Town Hall' business with their county town of Dumfries, including hospital visits, but this was not catered for until the 1950s—and then by bus. Indeed, the Third Statistical Account, that twentieth-century edition of a unique chronicle of Scottish parish history, commented as late as 1957 that a regular bus service had only just been established to link Langholm with its county town of Dumfries.

Passenger services were withdrawn from the branch on 15 June 1964, and freight from 18 September 1967. The last passenger train was seen off from Langholm by flute and pipe bands, one hundred years and 63 days after the service was introduced, according to a local newspaper report. (Presumably, this did not include the six-month hiatus caused by the Byreburn viaduct's collapse, thanks to the NBR's desperate need for any coal which might be underneath it!) This last service had to be reinforced, many Langholm citizens travelling as far as Canonbie and then walking home. It was a touching public gesture from a community which had been an innocent pawn in a railway power struggle a century earlier, before

In April 1963 at Riddings, St Margaret's-based 'A3' No 60037 Hyperion *hurries past the Langholm branch in the foreground with a northbound freight, the first two vehicles of which were non-corridor passenger stock. The locomotive was withdrawn eight months after this photograph was taken.* (Douglas Hume)

eventually being provided with a railway service so grudgingly.

If there is any lingering doubt about the rights and wrongs of the decision to site Langholm on a branch line, while providing the fells of Liddesdale with processions of Anglo-Scottish expresses, the following table from Elliot's thesis will provide confirmation, in comparing traffic receipts from Langholm and Newcastleton.

|  |  | Passengers booked | | Goods (tons) | |
|---|---|---|---|---|---|
|  |  | L'holm | N'ton | L'holm | N'ton |
| Jan-June | 1874 | 12,913 | 4,290 | 3,804 | 744 |
| " " | 1904 | 16,171 | 6,399 | 3,380 | 1,253 |
| " " | 1934 | 14,598 | 10,932 | 3,219 | 887 |

Obviously, Langholm was the busier of the two towns, as its population would suggest, with Newcastleton making up some ground on Langholm in the motor age. Nevertheless, it should be borne in mind that the latter town's passenger statistics were based on branch-line services, with comparatively few direct trains to Carlisle, never mind London; in contrast, Newcastleton had trains to and from St Pancras almost up to the 1970s.

When one bears in mind Elliot's contention that a Mosspaul line would have saved the NBR £100,000 in reaching Hawick from the south, it will be seen that the Liddesdale route was not only Langholm's loss. As a Caledonian legal counsel told the parliamentary inquiry in March 1859, it was

'quite comical to think of a railway running its main line through a desolate, uninhabited country, and putting the only place of any population and of any commerce upon a branch'.

# SARK BRIDGE, GRETNA

## West Coast Main Line

*Gretna Junction looking southwards in 1951, the year in which the station, visible beyond the Sark Bridge with its Border crossing signs, was closed.* (J. L. Stevenson collection)

The Border crossing at the Sark Bridge, just to the south-east of Gretna Green, carries two Anglo-Scottish routes. These part company immediately to the north of the bridge, the electrified West Coast (formerly Caledonian) Main Line heading northwards for Quintinshill, of 1915 infamy, and onwards to Carstairs, Glasgow, Edinburgh, and even farther north.

The facing turnout takes the former Glasgow & South Western line westwards to Dumfries, whence it continues northwards to Glasgow or, until 1965, west to Stranraer. Since the closure of this last-mentioned route, Stranraer trains now travel via Girvan, while even the GSWR main line itself is diminished in importance, becoming single at Gretna as far as Annan.

Gretna is more than just a tourist trap, trading on its traditional reputation for runaway weddings, and has an interesting railway history. It appeared many times in railway promoters' prospectuses during the 1840s Railway Mania; it was the nearest the Caledonian would tolerate the North British coming to Carlisle at one time, and it was temporarily the southern terminus for the misnamed Glasgow, Dumfries & Carlisle line.

So inextricably interwined were the early destinies of the two Glasgow-inspired railways, the Caledonian and the GD & C, that it will be convenient to consider them together for the purposes of this chapter.

Historian C. J. A. Robertson, whose work on the early history of Scotland's railways is of unequalled importance, has pointed out that public and commercial pressures for the crossing of the Anglo-Scottish border were largely confined to Scotland and the North of England. London did not see Scotland as being within its natural trading ambit, and, in any case, regular shipping contacts between the Thames and Scottish ports appeared to satisfy what demand there

*The Sark Bridge takes the weight of a down freight headed by 37 507 crossing from England to Scotland on 13 April 1988.* (Author)

was. Some merchants, however, saw these marine links as monopolistic and an increase in shipping rates in the 1830s made the concept of a long-distance railway more attractive, even at a time of unprecedented depression in trade.

Even by 1840, when the cities of Liverpool and Manchester, and Edinburgh and Glasgow, were connected to one another by iron rails, merchants from one of these twinned conurbations visiting the other would have to do so by road-coach or by sea. The great hills and fells of the Borderland and Lake District were as yet unchallenged by the steam engine. Not only had engineering problems to be overcome, but early traffic surveys suggested that only one Anglo-Scottish line would be likely to pay—yet it was plainly impossible to construct a line which would serve equally the Glasgow, Edinburgh, Lancashire and Tyneside interests.

With the Grand Junction Railway connecting Euston with many of the industrial centres of the north of England by 1837, it was natural for its promoters, and the growing community of railway speculators generally, to envisage a logical extension northwards, through Carlisle, and then splitting somewhere in the vicinity of Lanark, to serve the twin cities of Glasgow and Edinburgh, just as the Liverpool and Manchester lines did in the Crewe/Warrington area. Even more than a year before the opening of the GJR, its engineer, Joseph Locke, was carrying out a preliminary survey of the country north of Carlisle. The story goes that his journey took him no farther than the Beattock pass!

Beattock may have been something of a physical barrier for trains on the West Coast Main Line when it was eventually crossed by rails, at least during the age of steam traction, but it formed an even greater obstacle for railway promotion in the area. Apparently Locke was so appalled by the potential length and severity of an incline in the area that he immediately abandoned his survey of this Annandale route and turned to examining the logical alternative—a line from Gretna across the Solway moss to Dumfries, over the hill barrier in the Cumnock area and thence into Ayrshire. Apart from considerably easier gradients, this plan had the merit of serving more towns in passing and could connect with existing or projected lines in the Ayrshire area.

Locke's decision came as a shock and disappointment to the local MP for Dumfriesshire, John James Hope-Johnstone, who believed the railway would economically benefit his area while providing a much shorter journey from the south to both Glasgow and Edinburgh, in the latter case by some 50 miles over any Nithsdale/Ayrshire route. By assiduous campaigning, and given valuable time by a downturn in trade temporarily diluting enthusiasm for railway developments, Johnstone managed to convince Locke that he was being punctilious in his determination to avoid gradients. The famous engineer, a protégé of the Stephensons, was prepared to reconsider his opinion and produced a second report in November 1837.

This was scarcely a wholehearted championing of the Annandale

*This superb panning shot shows 'Jubilee' 4-6-0 No 45711* Courageous *racing down Beattock with a Glasgow express for Liverpool and Manchester in the 1950s. The descent of Beattock bank had worried its constructor Joseph Locke as much as its ascent, given the inadequate braking power of trains in the 1840s.* (D. A. Anderson)

route, but he did concede that an easing of the Beattock gradient was possible, while operating experience throughout the country suggested that a steam engine was capable of climbing inclines where cable assistance had previously been thought imperative. Of course, Locke correctly pointed out that *climbing* a gradient is only half the operating difficulty it entails. Equally, the *descent* of a long straight gradient presented brake-power problems which Locke was not slow to anticipate. As a result, while emphasizing the directness of the Annandale option, he was not emphatically in its favour. Indeed, one supporter of the rival Nithsdale route was recorded as saying that 'Mr Locke was writing against his own convictions'.

With not a yard of track yet straddling the two countries, it was perhaps opportune for the government of the day to step in. In 1839 a commission comprising Colonel Sir Frederick Smith of the Board of Trade and Professor Barlow of the Royal Military Academy was set up to report on railway communications between London, Glasgow, Edinburgh and Dublin. Two years later it reported on the future of Anglo-Scottish rail links, giving, as one historian has remarked, encouragement to nearly all the cross-Border promoters, with the exception of those hoping to make a central trunk line through the Cheviots from the north-east of England.

The Smith-Barlow commission gave broad, but not unqualified, approval to the Annandale party, with their idealistic conception of a 'Grand Junction' in rural Lanarkshire. However, the commissioners' reservations included the proviso that an East Coast line should be built if there was any delay in the commencement of a central West Coast line, in view of the time which would be needed for hills to be overcome (there was after all the question of Shap as well as Beattock). All this was of course on the assumption that there would be only one Anglo-Scottish line anyway, something which Locke believed to be commercial common sense (although that was arguably outside his remit as an engineer), but which was to be borne out by early traffic returns when train services did commence between England and Scotland. Tyneside's connections with Scotland were relegated by the commission to a roundabout route through Carlisle, possibly because of the existence of the line between these towns.

Ironically, the first line to cross the Border was to do so north of Berwick, its promoters correctly arguing that the Caledonian, as the Grand Junction/Annandale lobbies were now called, had failed to fulfil their intentions within the time-span thought reasonable by the Commissioners, doubtless due to the current recession in trade. Smith and Barlow had considered no fewer than eight routes (plus variations) across the Border, coming down in favour of the Annandale proposal. Much was to be made of this choice in subsequent inter-company propaganda, the later Caledonian lobby arguing that its was, as it were, the 'official' route into Scotland from the south, while the North British were to argue that their case was strengthened by the Annandale party's failure to construct a line within a reasonable period, as specified by Smith and Barlow. This argument equally kept the Nithsdale's group's hopes alive—they had made a poor showing before the commission, inexplicably failing to provide full or factual engineering data, despite being served by an engineer as experienced as John Miller. This was of course the same Scottish railway-builder we have already seen constructing the North British and who, at this time, had built the Edinburgh & Glasgow.

But the Nithsdale group, later known as the Glasgow, Dumfries & Carlisle Railway (and later still the Glasgow & South Western) found succour in the Caledonian's tardy approach to even commencing construction in southern Scotland. Indeed, the slowness of the victorious Annandale party in consolidating their victory by beginning proper building operations was even to tempt the North British to speculate with its Hawick branch farther south, at one time with GD & C co-operation. The Caledonian was allowing trouble to pile up for itself, although delay was perhaps inevitable, given the nature of the undertaking.

'An English railway in disguise,' is the opinion of economic historian C. J. A. Robertson of the Caledonian, which was, after all, linked into the fortunes of the Lancaster & Carlisle, itself the northern extension of the Grand Junction. The fact that 77 per cent of the Caledonian's capital came from south of the Border meant that the stockholders there probably placed greater emphasis on first conquering the English fells to reach Carlisle from the south than in staking out newly-won territory north of the Border city.

As late as 1844 the Caledonian Railway records show that Locke was still offering advice on the outline of the projected route. As well as recommending that a municipally-backed committee should decide on the location of the through Carlisle station, he appeared, in a report dated 5 August, to suggest taking the line westwards from Gretna and then northwards through Annan, as opposed to Gretna-Lockerbie (hitherto 'Annandale' had referred to the northern area of that river; this would have had no rail connections with the town of the same name standing near the mouth of the River Annan on the Solway Firth). His report suggested that Beattock bank could be built at a reduced gradient and three lengthy viaducts avoided. In other words, the Caledonian planning as late as 1844 was not exactly well-advanced, an impression reinforced by Locke's appeal for standard gauge to be adopted for its construction!

This prevarication was not the only factor keeping the GD & C in being; the passing of the North British Railway's 1844 Act virtually guaranteed that there would be more than one railway crossing the Border, and with Edinburgh being connected with England through Berwick, the argument for a 'central' line north from Carlisle was weakened. Not only that, but with Edinburgh receipts on the Caledonian likely to be diminished, and the lack of intermediate

*Engineer Joseph Locke considered Beattock pass an insurmountable obstacle for the railway built northwards from Gretna, and although he later modified his opinion, this steep natural incline gave credibility to the alternative Nithsdale route (the GSWR), and created decades of bitter rivalry between the companies and their staffs. In this fine shot, Class '8P' 'Pacific' No 46225* Duchess of Gloucester *is seen making smoke as she climbs the 'insurmountable' bank with a Birmingham-Glasgow express around 1960.* (D. A. Anderson)

traffic from the Annandale route where there was no sizeable habitation between Carlisle and Lanark, the Dumfries route was made to look even more attractive. The seeds were planted for what became a fairly bitter rivalry between the two factions north of Carlisle, one which continued almost until 1923.

March 1844 saw the publication of both the Caledonian and the GD & C prospectuses. The latter company had now established that its proposed line would stretch southwards from Kilmarnock and not Ayr, and by the end of the year received substantial financial support from the Edinburgh & Glasgow, a line which would obviously benefit if the North British and the Nithsdale lines were the only ones to be built across the Border. As already seen, in 1845 the NBR, GD & C, E & G and Ayrshire Railways formed an alliance to fight the Caledonian in Parliament, and ensure an Edinburgh-Carlisle route via Hawick. On the face of it, the Edinburgh & Glasgow's membership of this particular syndicate appears illogical as it would remove the possibility of Edinburgh to north-west of England traffic through Glasgow; Robertson believes that their greater fear was that the Caledonian, traversing so much unremunerative countryside south of the Clyde Valley, would be forced to compete for Edinburgh-Glasgow traffic via Carstairs. That this did in fact subsequently happen, and more damagingly for the Caledonian than its northern rival, is yet another fibre in the twisted knot of railway promotions of the time.

In 1845 came the parliamentary defeat of this alliance; the Caledonian lobby swept all before them, almost certainly because of sympathetic friends in the Cabinet, while the North British had rather fallen foul of the Earl of Dalhousie, at the Board of Trade, in its takeover of the Edinburgh & Dalkeith line. Support for the Caledonian from the Scottish capital was cleverly ensured by allowing the Edinburgh and Leith Water Company to lay a conduit beside the proposed Carstairs-Edinburgh branch eastwards from Cobbinshaw, the railway company to be allowed access to this as required. Suffice to say that the Caledonian/Annandale supporters had been handed a second chance to build across the Border.

The Caledonian's enabling Act received the Royal Assent on 31 July 1845, giving the company 'the command of the general railway traffic of Scotland'—confirming that this was the 'official' Anglo-Scottish railway. In their hour of victory the Directors felt that they could tolerate what their company's Minutes called a rival 'Kilmarnock, Dumfries, and Carlisle line' provided it was no more than of local importance. Indeed, the Caledonian made it clear that it would not be averse to running operations over such a line itself; it had failed to receive parliamentary approval for two lines based on Dumfries. One would have headed towards Edinburgh and Glasgow northwards (presumably taking the picturesque but forbidding Dalveen pass to Elvanfoot), while the other would have connected Dumfries with Carlisle through Annan and Gretna. The company records show that

**Far right** *Beattock summit is near for '8P' 'Pacific' No 46253 City of St Albans heading the northbound 'Royal Scot' late in the 1950s. The earliest, probably token, efforts to construct the Caledonian's Anglo-Scottish main line took place near here in 1846, only for the company to find that they had to pay customs duties on importing the wheelbarrows and tools from England!* (D. A. Anderson)

the county town of the area was something of a fixation for the Caledonian, which was determined to get there somehow, despite this being its only rebuff at Westminster. In mid-1847, when staffing plans were being drawn up for the new line, Gretna was to be regarded as a '1st Class Station' with a Station Keeper on 30 shillings (£1.50) per week, plus a free house, assisted by a porter, and, significantly, the list includes the suffix 'N.B. Two signal men night and day will be required when the Dumfries line is opened'.

Having failed to take action after being given the go-ahead by Smith and Barlow—no prospectus was issued, no bill presented to Westminster—this time the opportunity was seized. Symbolic clearing of the ground at Beattock summit immediately began, action which somewhat backfired on the company. Within a few months the Caledonian was faced with a bill for customs duties on the import of 'mud waggons, barrows, and planks'.

Fifty locomotives and 400 carriages were the rolling-stock requirements decided upon by the directors of Scotland's newest, and designedly greatest, railway, but by the following year 50 engines were only thought sufficient for passenger services alone, orders being placed by the end of 1846 for these plus 30 goods engines and three 'bank' engines, one of them to be purchased from the Greenock Railway. By this time the Caledonian had agreed to work over at least part of the Scottish Central system northwards, so the line's horizons were broadening.

Initially, an order for 15 engines and tenders was placed with Jones & Potts (seven to be delivered by July 1847, the rest six months later, at a cost of £2,200 each). Jones and Potts was a Lancashire firm at Newton-le-Willows, specializing in Allan-type locomotives which became very much a characteristic of early Caledonian operations. The neighbouring firm of Charles Tayleur also appears in the company records; by 1847 this firm's name had changed to the Vulcan Foundry. Five additional locomotives were considered necessary for operation by February 1848, but the amount of coaching stock ordered was appreciably less than earlier forecast; 35 coaches were under construction in July 1846 for delivery at Carlisle.

A £1,275,000 construction contract was awarded to Mackenzie Stevenson and Brassey in February 1845 to build the line from Carlisle to the junction with the Wishaw & Coltness (the northern stretch of the line to Glasgow was to be over the course of two established mineral lines, very much like the North British using the Edinburgh & Dalkeith as the basis for the northern section for the Hawick line). Work was not really under way until the summer of 1846 when men and materials were expected to be released from the Lancaster & Carlisle workings to augment locally-recruited labour, believed to already consist of around 3,500 men.

Bad weather in the early months of the year slowed construction from Carlisle towards the Scottish Border. In February, Errington, Locke's second-in-command, reported that 'designs have been fur-

*Beloved by a now grown-up generation of Hornby-Dublo model railway owners, Polmadie 'Pacific' No 46232* Duchess of Montrose *climbs Beattock bank with a Birmingham-Glasgow working around 1960.* (D. A. Anderson)

nished for the bridges over the Eden and the Esk, and when the floods subside these bridges will be immediately commenced'. By mid-1846, however, the Directors were asking for work to be accelerated, and, as with the NBR, were finding the need for an enforcing order on their unruly navvies. A riot at Lockerbie had to be put down by a force of militia riding from Carlisle, while one labourer, a John Smith, was awarded the princely sum of £5 compensation for losing both legs in an accident, also at Lockerbie. (Two years later the redoubtable Mr Smith had engaged a solicitor in Dumfries and the company was being forced to offer him a job of gatekeeper or something suited to his handicapped state.) By October the Dumfriesshire police asked the company for a 'lock-up house' to be built at the latter's expense at Woodhouse; the Caledonian Directors cannily decided that work was so far advanced on that particular section that no further trouble could be expected from the labourers there. In January 1847, however, they were sufficiently worried about the problem to allocate £100 for the 'religious instruction' of the navvies.

No fewer than 10,500 men and 860 horses were by now engaged on building the new line. Five miles of trackbed were prepared on the English side of the Border by the summer of 1846, with a temporary bridge already existing over the Eden and that over the Esk expected to be completed that year. The stations officially planned in October

1846 for the line as far north as the Edinburgh-Glasgow junction were:

| 1st Class | 2nd Class |
|---|---|
| Springfield (Gretna) | Rockliffe |
| Lockerbie | Kirkpatrick |
| Beattock | Kirtle Bridge (sic) |
| Abington | Ecclefechan |
| | Hangingshaw |
| | Wamphray |
| | Elvanfoot |
| | Crawford |
| | Lamington |
| | Symington |
| | Thankerton |
| | Float (Carstairs) |

This was more than a fair share of stations for some 72 miles of fairly sparsely populated countryside; nowadays, only Lockerbie station exists on this stretch south of Carstairs. Other local districts which the Caledonian were anxious to accommodate in their plans were Annan—to be reached from two different directions—and Dumfries, to be approached from the north only.

There is no doubt that the Gretna area, sited in the 'Debatable Lands' traditionally contested between Englishman and Scot, became a veritable cockpit of inter-Company rivalry in the late 1840s (see the accompanying map). Obviously, this was where any line from Niths-dale and points north would have to turn southwards towards Carlisle, unless an attempt to cross the Solway was envisaged. As a result, the Caledonian not only located its Gretna station in England, where it was not over-convenient for this Scottish village, but intended to use the area as a bulwark to secure the northern approach to Carlisle for itself.

In December 1846 the Caledonian planned a double-tracked Y-shaped branch from Mossband, south of Gretna, to Canonbie and Langholm. The former destination would give access to the Duke of Buccleuch's mines, but the latter may have had primarily a strategic value, the Caledonian Directors deciding, in the face of mounting costs unrelieved by any revenue, 'to go on at present till the decision of the North British Company is known as to the Hawick and Carlisle extension'. In other words, the Caledonian hoped to 'occupy the ground' to block any such line through the logical route of Langholm. This project was costed at nearly a quarter of a million pounds, indicating the importance attached to keeping the NB out of Carlisle. Similarly, there was a 4½-mile line proposed from Crookdyke (near Rockliffe) to Longtown planned also as a blocking manoeuvre (there would have been a triangular junction south-west of Longtown with the Langholm/Canonbie branch) but a 12½-mile branch projected from Longtown to Milton was not presented to Parliament for

*Proposed lines around Gretna, 1847.*

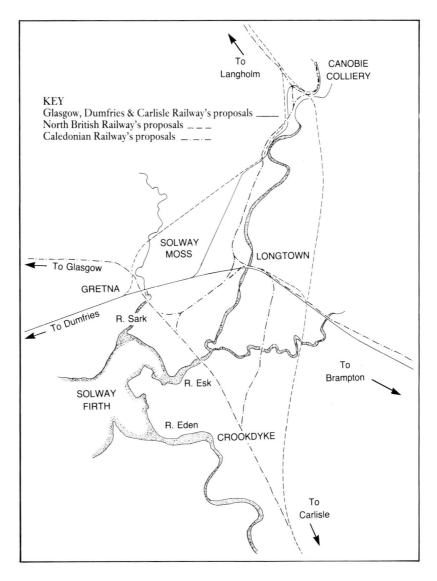

KEY
Glasgow, Dumfries & Carlisle Railway's proposals _____
North British Railway's proposals _ _ _
Caledonian Railway's proposals _ _·_ _

approval. A possible 14-mile £180,000 single-line branch to Dumfries from the north-eastern direction was, unusually, only to be considered after local residents had been sounded out.

But it was not only the North British which the Caledonian was fighting. As already shown, the Nithsdale faction had neither been vanquished by the findings of the Smith-Barlow commission, nor strengthened by the Caledonian's failure to mobilize its forces after that victory.

The company had begun as an offshoot of the Ayrshire railway lobby, the provosts of Paisley, Kilmarnock, Dumfries and Ayr appearing on the stockholders' prospectus, although, as C. J. A. Robertson puts it, 'sadly the Lord Provost of Glasgow was committed to the Caledonian'. The scheme's supporters did not receive the

Royal Assent for their line until 31 July 1846, and at once decided to lease their still-unbuilt line to the Glasgow, Kilmarnock & Ayr Railway, with amalgamation planned for the time of the opening of the main line. However, the GD & C Act contained a crippling handicap, which in turn underlined the Caledonian's pre-eminence in the Westminster corridors of power.

The rival Nithsdale line could only be built as far east as Gretna if the final 8 miles of it were operated by the Caledonian! It hardly seems worthwhile in retrospect for Parliament to have passed the Act at all, since this effectively would kill the Nithsdale party's chances of operating as a through Anglo-Scottish route. The Directors of the Glasgow, Dumfries & Carlisle (the Carlisle part of it now somewhat academic) informed their shareholders that this running powers clause was 'objectionable', going on to tell them:

'All the Ayr and Dumfriesshire traffic which is to be worked as far as Annan by the Glasgow and Ayr Railway Company, shall at that point be handed over to a different Company who seek the Lease professedly for the purpose of obstructing the traffic. Your Directors cannot believe that when the nature and effect of this Clause are understood that Parliament will allow the interests of these Counties and of the public to be sacrificed to the fears of the Caledonian Company lest their through traffic be interfered with.'

Rubbing salt into the freshly inflicted wound, the Caledonian decided to prepare for a formal application to Parliament for running powers to Annan, while also planning a 7-mile double-track branch northwards from there to rejoin its main line at Ecclefechan. The GD & C was asked if they would consider a joint station at Annan, an idea its Board refused even to discuss. Meanwhile, the Caledonian was cheerfully planning to oppose the other company's plans for branches to Canonbie, Langholm and Milton, east of Brampton. (The Newcastle & Carlisle had enquired of the GD & C late in 1846 about a Portpatrick line, making Tyneside traffic with Ireland a possibility.) Unfortunately for the Nithsdale supporters, the House of Lords had already refused a GD & C branch to Canonbie, preferring a Caledonian proposal.

The map on p107 sums up the tangled welter of railways planned for the area immediately south and east of Gretna, including for the sake of completeness those lines not empowered by Parliament up to 1847, but illustrating the strategic importance of the area immediately east of the Solway. A glance will show that the Caledonian's branches running north-eastwards from Crookdyke and from the Mossband area just south of Gretna were duplicatory; in particular the former's only probable function was to force the North British to stay well east of the Solway, and perhaps to discourage any GD & C attempt to curve southwards from their projected Brampton line. In September 1847 the latter company was loftily informed by their successful CR rivals that they need not try to establish operations east of Gretna 'beyond the legitimate boundary of their Railway as indicated by the decision of Parliament'. Yet there would surely have been some justification for the two companies already allied against the Caledonian at Westminster, to have considered a joint approach to the Border City, where in July 1847, incidentally, the Lancaster & Carlisle was highly displeased with the Caledonian's tardiness in paying its share towards the new joint station. However, by that time the NBR's Carlisle extension had been defeated in Parliament and the Nithsdale lobby was fighting to remove the tourniquet the Caledonian had placed on their own line east of Annan.

Another feature of the map is the extraordinary attention paid to Canonbie. Three different companies projected three lines to this coal-producing area, owned by the Duke of Buccleuch. That worthy owner could, it seemed, look forward to moving his minerals northwards by the North British, north or south by the Caledonian, or south and south-westwards by the Glasgow, Dumfries & Carlisle. Interestingly, despite his support in London for the furtherance of Caledonian interests, the Duke assured the GD & C in the autumn of 1846 that he would give preference to that company's attempt to reach Canonbie, on the somewhat gentlemanly grounds that they were the first to approach him. Similarly, he assured them of his abhorrence of the Caledonian's stifling Annan-Gretna powers. The price the company had to pay for this ducal support was to build a tunnel in Nithsdale to hide the line from his seat of Drumlanrig Castle. The tunnel, plus its approaches, was given out to tender for £112,000 for a 8,600-yard site.

Just to further complicate the already twisted skein of lines approved or proposed for the area of the Esk basin, in November

*Two tracks no longer diverge from the West Coast Main Line at Gretna Junction as in this photograph taken 6 August 1966. Passing on the former Caledonian main line, and about to cross the Sark Bridge into England, is 'Black Five' No 44677 heading the 11.35 Glasgow (Central)-Manchester (Victoria) relief express.*
(Douglas Hume)

1846 the Caledonian suggested building its own link line to the Newcastle & Carlisle at Brampton, obviously with Newcastle-Glasgow traffic in mind. Within three weeks the English Company had politely 'reserved to themselves to deal with Brampton'. Such a line would not have been so very far removed from an earlier concept, a waggonway planned in 1825 by a group of Dumfriesshire landowners who hoped to connect Port Annan (presumably Annan Waterfoot) with Brampton—evidence yet again that the Gretna area, through which such a line would have to pass, was more than just a target destination for eloping couples. This most westerly terrestrial crossing of the Border was a vital strategic site for railway companies to command, and at the end of the 1840s it was indisputably the Caledonian who dominated proceedings.

But what of the inhabitants of Gretna themselves? Their station was to be built immediately south of the Sark bridge, but there was a delay before access to the chosen site was gained in May 1847, and the station's foundations were not laid until the end of the month. The booking office was scheduled to be ready by August but little else was expected to be finished. Ironically, by June 1848 the citizens of Springfield, part of this much-targeted rail-centre, were complaining about the inconvenient siting of their station. They had a point—it was in a different country! This was no mere academic point; with the retail price of spirits lower north of the Border, Gretna villagers walking to 'their' station would be subject to customs searches, something which also afflicted trains on the Edinburgh-Berwick line.

However, in all this territorial consolidation, the Caledonian was sowing the seeds of what very nearly became its own destruction. Significantly, in November 1846, while planning a veritable spider's web of railways sited on the Anglo-Scottish border to Annan, Canonbie, Langholm, Longtown and Brampton, the Board was told that it would be financially impossible to lease the Edinburgh & Glasgow line. Historically, this was a disastrous omission; rivalry with the E & G was to bring the Caledonian to its knees within a few years, while the final amalgamation between that Company and the North British Railway in 1865—surely always a distinct possibility—was to present the Caledonian with a powerful business rival in the densely-populated West of Scotland. Indeed, the NBR was to become the biggest Scottish Company, in terms of track miles if not in prestige; this could have been prevented if the Caledonian had leased the Edinburgh & Glasgow's main line and eventually purchased it, instead of committing early capital in speculative branch-line development in the Border area.

Ironically, just as the North British frittered away much of its early financial resources on branch lines, so the Caledonian precipitated a crisis for itself by doing much the same. Not only that, but a vast financial incentive was promised to the contractors for an early completion of the works; this with contributions from the Caledonian's southern neighbours. A £70,000 bonus was offered if the line could be opened throughout to Edinburgh and Glasgow by 1 November 1847. This inducement was offered in the previous February but in only a month it became obvious that neither the Glasgow terminus nor the Cleghorn cutting could possibly be ready in time, while a temporary terminus was already planned for Edinburgh, a city which was not to see the Caledonian at its most opulent for another half-century.

Not that opulence was exactly the keyword as the winter of 1847-8 approached with no trains yet running throughout the length of the Caledonian. Just as the North British was finding the going heavy in the Border hills, so the Caledonian was fighting for financial oxygen. Some £100,000 capital was needed for the branch-line projects; significantly these began to lose their priority status. While the Canonbie line was ordered to be 'staked out' in September 1847, no work was to be undertaken meanwhile on the Crookdyke-Longtown line. Similarly, nothing was to be done with the Langholm branch if the Duke of Buccleuch was not pressing for this to be built. By October the Board 'resolved to suspend all works not absolutely essential to the opening of the main line'. This was to include a year's suspension of any promotion of a line to Dumfries, while the Brampton project was virtually written off.

Two Directors were despatched to London to raise credit if they could (meeting with 'doubtful success'); in the following month the Commercial bank stopped the company's overdraft at £50,000. Yet not long before, the Directors were pondering such niceties as the appearance of staff uniforms (to resemble those of the LNWR): guards and stationmasters to wear silver thistle badges, while the buttons would incorporate a thistle motif with the company's name round the circumference. If nothing else, the Caledonian had style, even in adversity.

Obviously, the company was desperate to begin operations, even although Beattock bank was still not suitable for traffic. It was decided to have a formal opening journey—from Carlisle to Beattock station only, very much for the benefit of the shareholders and the company's allies to the south—on Thursday 9 September 1847, with full traffic operation starting the following day.

At 11.20 that Thursday, in rain which was to continue throughout the day, a five-coach train arrived at Carlisle station from the north, bearing the Caledonian's Directors. (They had presumably travelled southwards the previous day by a mixture of road and rail, although the Board minutes are silent on this point.) Waiting at Carlisle's Crown Square were the city's mayor and a party from the Lancaster & Carlisle Railway. The local *Carlisle Patriot* recorded that four more coaches were added to the formation and that departure for Beattock took place around noon, a stop being made at Gretna to pick up Sir James Graham and a local cleric. The Border had now been crossed by train at a second location.

The 40 miles to Beattock were accomplished in two hours, the passengers promptly tucking into a 'cold collation', accompanied by toasts and speeches. At four o'clock the special train returned southwards bearing its English-based guests, reaching Carlisle in a slightly faster time than northbound. It was a low-key event, quite clearly geared to convincing the Caledonian's southern friends and investors that progress was being made. But the day's heavy rain was not inappropriate; there were storm clouds ahead for the company before it could open throughout between Carlisle and Edinburgh/ Glasgow, and indeed, even after that time.

One interesting footnote to this partial railway opening, with traffic operating only between Carlisle and Beattock station, was that the Caledonian soon found it was having to start its trains earlier than timetabled. Northbound passengers arriving at Carlisle from London discovered that Carlisle was in a different time-zone, and had to adjust their watches! It seems incredible nowadays to realize that Britain did not adopt a standard time (Greenwich Mean Time) until 1884; prior to the railway age it was almost physically impossible for a traveller to move in any short interval between towns with different time-zones; from now on the problem would only be solved by the GPO insisting on London time being adopted. Thus the following advertisement was placed in the *Glasgow Herald* by the Caledonian only ten weeks after opening between Carlisle and Beattock:

'In consequence of instructions received from the GPO, it is intended, on and after the 1st day of December next, to adopt LONDON TIME on the Caledonian Railway. From the above date the MAIL will leave Carlisle for the North at 9.16 am and 9.16 pm and leave Beattock for the south at 1.48 pm and 1.29 pm.

London time—in advance of local time—12 minutes at Carlisle; 12 at Edinburgh; 17 at Glasgow.'

Intending passengers were advised to subtract the minutes indicated from the timetable already published, although it is not clear if the starting times listed above were local or London time, something passengers would now make a point of establishing, 'otherwise passengers will be too late for the train', as the advertisement concluded.

Friday 15 February 1848 was an eventful day in the history of the Caledonian Railway—its first day of operations between Scotland's two largest cities and Carlisle. As was the case with the opening of the first cross-Border main line on the east of the country, a special pre-opening journey was arranged for the Directors and selected guests and journalists four days before the actual opening, but there was to be no junketing for the line's Directors. For they must have been aware of an imminent meeting a few days hence where they would be locked in a Boardroom drama which threatened the very existence of Scotland's newest railway.

But this did not concern the *Glasgow Herald*'s correspondent on Monday 11 February as he took his place in the first train to leave Glasgow's Townhead station for Beattock. Neither the company's records nor the newspaper report indicate precisely why a longer 'press run', perhaps all the way to Carlisle, could not have been undertaken; it was not as if, as at Dunbar in 1846, Beattock the previous autumn, or at Dumfries six months later, that time had to be allowed for a ceremonial meal with appropiate speeches. As we shall see, Scotland's mightiest railway was christened with less ceremony than either the North British or the 24-mile Dumfries to Gretna line.

Prompt at 09.45 the Caledonian's first train pulled out 'and proceeded by the Garnkirk and Wishaw and Coltness lines (which are already well known to the citizens of Glasgow) to Overtown Station'. While travelling southwards from that point, the reporter was amused to see in the Clyde Valley both south-bound and north-bound mail-coaches, the guard of one of which resolutely refused to acknowledge the waves and cheers from the train's passengers. At Beattock station—the descent of Beattock which had so worried Joseph Locke did not excite the attention of a newspaper representative who was among the first members of the public to experience it—who should meet the train but the Railway's chairman Hope-Johnstone and none other than Locke himself.

Little time was spent here—Beattock in midwinter has perhaps a limited appeal—before the northbound journey began. At Float station (which the paper remarked might be renamed Carstairs), the Edinburgh portion was uncoupled; this had reached the junction first on the outward journey, another correspondent being particularly inspired by the beauty of Cobbinshaw reservoir. The paper carried a description of the first-class coaching stock which is worth recording here:

'Both First and Second Class carriages are in every way handsome and commodious . . . [the First Class] are painted lake colour on the outside, and highly varnished. Inside they are 5 ft 10 inches high and each department is six feet by seven in dimension. They are fitted up in blue colour, cloth on the cushions, morocco elbows, silk window blinds and layings, and Brussels carpet . . . the wood work is mahogany highly polished, and the topsides and roof are covered with cream coloured oilcloth. Above the window, strips of stained glass have been introduced, which give the carriages a light and cheerful appearance.'

On this February Monday it appeared that the Directors transferred to the Edinburgh portion, and four days later, at the Company's office at 122 Princes Street, the Board was presented with a 'Bill of Extras' from its construction contractors for a cool quarter of a million pounds.

Earlier in the month the Caledonian had been offered the chance to buy out their contractors' existing agreements for approximately £100,000 but instead had offered £15,000 for workers' wages at six sites where works were still being undertaken. This represented almost all the funds the Company had in hand; obviously they desperately awaited traffic revenues, if only to make the banks look more favourably on their credit needs. At this opening-day meeting, the contractors were not to be put off so easily; nor could the Caledonian lose sight of the fact that the same firm had been enjoined to undertake basic operations and day-to-day maintenance after opening.

Fortunately for the beleaguered company, their consulting engineer Joseph Locke came to the rescue. Estimating that the real debt to the contractors for the still not fully operational railway (the *Herald*'s reporter noted single-line operations at Beattock summit cutting and the line northwards to Castlecary was incomplete) was probably £91,187, he suggested the Caledonian consider offering to pay this in instalments. Station designer William Tite may have made himself somewhat unpopular at this point by suggesting that some £6,400 had been overlooked for station construction work, but meanwhile the contractors refused to consider any offer made unofficially, without the full weight of approval of the Board. The interlocutions of Locke and Tite appear to have allowed the Directors—no strangers to financial crises by now—time to rally their wits. Following Locke's initiative in haggling the contractors' price downwards, the Caledonian Directors convinced themselves that the real sum owing was £20,587, and that this could be written off as the contractors had been able to salvage so many materials for use elsewhere! They then cleverly offered a new seven-month contract to finish the works for £90,000 to be paid between then and August! The maintenance contract was to stand for seven years. It was a masterly escape from a major crisis. There would be more, but at least now the Company could point out that its trains were moving.

'The running of the trains is unusually exact for a new establishment,' Locke informed the Board in May, setting a tradition that was to be followed for the next 75 years of Caledonian rail operations. These could hardly have been aided by the lack of locomotive facilities at the Glasgow terminus, where £1,500 had to be hastily voted for the building of a water tank, shed accommodation and forges. Two more goods engines had to be purchased within a week of opening, while Carstairs Junction station—a name which Edinburgh citizens were to come to view with less than affection—was to have a £200 passenger shed (presumably the overall roof which lasted until 1913), but definitely no refreshment facilities!

Relations with other railways were still of major importance. The Caledonian, in claiming to be *the* Scottish railway, made arrangements for the leasing of the Scottish Midland, Dundee & Newtyle and Dundee & Arbroath lines, creating the prospect of through services to Dundee and Aberdeen, even though the connection through to the Larbert area via the Castlecary branch was not yet open.

Failure to lease the Edinburgh & Glasgow was to haunt the Caledonian; no sooner had they fixed fares between these cities of 6s (30p) for first class, 4/6d (22½p) second, and 3s (15p) for third, than they had to reduce them to 4s, 3s, and 2/6d within three months (all single fares—the Caledonian, when enquiring about the possibility of issuing return tickets on its system, was warned by the LNWR, Lancashire & Yorkshire and GWR to avoid doing so). The reduction was in reply to the fares of the Edinburgh & Glasgow, a company already honed by competition with the canals across the central Scottish isthmus. The E & G had a shorter route, although journey times were not vitally important to a population brought up in an age of horse transport, so fare-cutting was a legitimate means of competition.

Unfortunately, the Caledonian was soon appalled to find that the E & G was prepared to cut its fares to London as well, despite the longer distance via Edinburgh! On 21 July the new company decided to contact its ally south of Carlisle to ascertain if a London-Glasgow fare reduction was possible, provided this was fairly divided between the two companies. As if that was not enough, the Board learned that even the Glasgow-Newcastle fare by the East Coast was lower; the Caledonian and the Newcastle & Carlisle agreed in February 1848 on a 31/6d (£1.57½p) first class fare, 11s (55p) of this being due to the English Company.

In April 1848 a solution to the last of these problems raised its head; the chairman of the Newcastle & Carlisle was about to retire and one of the Caledonian's Directors, Kelso-based John Hodgson Hinde, MP for Newcastle, believed that the newly-active Scottish Company would be an ideal operator for the line. He surmised that the obvious rival, George Hudson, would be unable to gain control as this would present a monopoly situation, so the Caledonian, mindful of the results of its failure to take over the E & G, allowed itself to be persuaded to apply for a lease of the line. The company's first offer was dismissed as 'inadequate', but considerable negotiation went on in the month of May. This resulted in a Caledonian offer which was received too late and an injunction was immediately sought to prevent Hudson taking over. Obviously, the Scottish company was in no fit state to take over such a concern, which in 1862 passed into the maw of the North Eastern Railway, incidentally allowing that York-based company the opportunity of negotiating running-powers from Berwick to Edinburgh and even beyond—had the Caledonian succeeded in taking over the Newcastle & Carlisle, it would presumably not have agreed to allow the NBR running powers from Hexham to Newcastle and the North British would not have been saddled with the October 1862 agreement it spent so many years trying to extricate itself from. Of course, all that is hypothetical speculation; suffice to say that the Caledonian was not to gain entry to Tyneside.

\*　　\*　　\*

If the Caledonian in its opening year was beleaguered by contractors, banks and more experienced competitors, it hardly made it more sympathetic to the interests of its by now overshadowed neighbour west of Gretna, the GD & C, and it is now appropriate to examine that company's fortunes.

The stifling running powers which the Caledonian was granted west of Gretna do not appear to have been formalized, probably because these would have to be incorporated in a parliamentary bill for branch-line expansion in the Border area, and the Company was quick to cut back on its branch-line legislation plans when economies had to be made. Even the Caledonian's southern allies had been somewhat taken aback by the deadly effective means of curtailing its rival by such an arrangement, and with the Duke of Buccleuch similarly arraigned against the idea of the Caledonian choking off traffic from Ayrshire and Dumfriesshire, the Nithsdale lobby was able to proceed with building its own line, the second intended to connect Glasgow with England.

Ironically, the records show that the section west of Gretna towards Dumfries was built more quickly than the line northwards from the latter town, although that might be expected, given the respective topographies. Just as the North British and Caledonian had found the effects of the 1847-8 recession to be crippling, so did the GD & C. By July 1848 it had decided to stop all work north of Dumfries, a decree which seems to have proved impossible to put into effect, probably for contractual reasons. The Drumlanrig contract was proving to be a major problem; construction work immediately north and south was virtually complete, but work on this by now notorious tunnel was most certainly not, the appointed contractor transferring the work to another, with the Board's approval.

There were fewer problems east of Dumfries, and preparations were made in the summer of 1848 to begin train operations on that 24-mile stretch through Annan to Gretna. Arrangements were made for locomotive coke to be delivered at Gretna, while engine drivers and firemen recruited in Glasgow were even offered removal expenses, and Edmondson tickets were to be applied for. But would the Caledonian co-operate?

At the midsummer half-yearly shareholders' meeting in Glasgow's Star Hotel, 23 August was appointed as the opening date of this so-far ill-starred line 'when the trains will run in connection with those on the Caledonian line at Gretna'. Correspondence was exchanged with the larger company, and the GD & C prepared locomotive and carriage facilities at Gretna even before building a station. By the autumn the rolling-stock accommodation was being insured for £1,000, 'the carriages and wagons therein for a further £1,000'. There were almost certainly leased from the Glasgow, Kilmarnock & Ayr.

By this time the line was opened, with no clear record as to how traffic was exchanged at the Gretna end. On the Monday of the opening week the line's Directors travelled by the Caledonian from Glasgow to Gretna where, according to a newspaper correspondent, 'they found an engine and carriages upon their own line'. This train took them to Dumfries, the Directors inspecting the 24-mile line as they went. There were 28 over-bridges and 31 under-bridges, but no major engineering features apart from the viaduct at Annan.

A special train for 200 invited guests left Dumfries on the Tuesday morning to the peal of bells and the cheers of thousands. The Dumfries station was not ready, a temporary terminus being improvized on the east of the town, whence Annan was reached in only 31 minutes. Here the entire Town Council was waiting on the platform to greet the first train, with the masts of assembled sailing ships visible in the harbour nearby. At Annan a band struck up 'Blue Bonnets over the Border', although on reaching Gretna it became obvious that the Border would remain uncrossed on this occasion. With the travelling band now playing 'Wooed and married and a'' (thought suitable for Gretna's romantic associations) the travellers were able to view the incomplete station near the parish church. A swift return was made to Dumfries.

Here a 'sumptuous collation' awaited the guests, followed by what must have been a bewildering succession of toasts. One of these was, interestingly, 'The Caledonian Railway', whose sole representative, a Mr Monteith of Carstairs, apologized for his company's poor representation. He was cheered to the echo as he wished the new railway well, his speech stressing its local impact, and cleverly punned that Gretna might prove to be a venue for a marriage of understanding between the two rival companies. The ceremonial meal broke up about 4 o'clock, but Dumfries celebrated into the hours of darkness, bells pealing, a bonfire burning in one of the main streets, and fireworks bursting in the night sky.

Despite Mr Monteith's hopes for a reconciliation between the Caledonian and GSWR (as it was already referred to by the *Glasgow*

*Once the Glasgow, Dumfries & Carlisle Railway's enforced terminus, Gretna Green was the most conveniently situated of the town's three stations, although little business seems evident in this shot of '5MT' No 44902 calling with the 18.00 Carlisle-Glasgow (St Enoch) stopping train on 25 May 1964. Note the unusual headlamp code and the tracks stretching southwards to the curve south to Gretna Junction.* (Douglas Hume)

*Gretna Green station looking westwards in the 1920s.* (J. L. Stevenson collection)

*Herald*), there was of course no question of the latter's trains running through to Carlisle, and as the smaller company's station was incomplete at the time of opening—it was still incomplete three months later—there is a possibility (not confirmed in the Board minutes) of the Caledonian station being used. But if the Dumfries Company believed that there might be a relaxation in the Caledonian's attitude, an unpleasant surprise was in store.

In October of that year, the GD & C Directors asked the larger Company to stop their 'Southern Express' train at Gretna, to allow a connection with their own Dumfries-bound train. The Caledonian Directors decided that they 'could not afford the time' to stop the 16.15 down, which previously stopped at Gretna, despite the obvious prospect of encouraging connecting traffic which would of course also benefit their own Company. As a sop, however, the GD & C services were to be listed in the Caledonian timetables—surely a perverse decision in view of the previous one.

Running powers into Carlisle were not granted to the GSWR until 15 February 1853, initially for five years, although confirmed as permanent in 1865. Tolls at the outset were 1s (5p) per ton for local goods, with an extra penny per ton for freight for destinations south of Carlisle, where the Caledonian's goods station was to be shared. For passenger rates there was to be a mileage charge calculated on 9 miles (the actual distance from Gretna to Carlisle) for local passengers, and 12 miles for those travelling beyond Carlisle.

While 1848 may have been the year when the Nithsdale group saw their railway, or at least part of it, bearing traffic, there was little respite for the Company from the realities of the economic depress-

*Gretna Green signalbox, just west of the now closed station, commands the view of '5MT' No 44796 heading south with a mineral train on 6 August 1966.* (Douglas Hume)

ion. By November the Secretary was advising the Directors 'that the Funds for meeting the company's expenses had been exhausted for some days'. The decision was taken to request £72,000 of previously promised capital from their associated Company, the Glasgow, Kilmarnock & Ayr. This proved to be a tenuous transaction; as soon as the money was received two months later, the Ayrshire Company immediately asked for it back as a loan! Apparently, this was agreed to, with debenture loans expected by this time, but 1849 opened with a further £368,656 required to complete the Dumfries-Sanquhar section, and an additional £174,150 for the section north of there into Ayrshire.

It would be fascinating, but beyond the remit of this book, to examine the continuing vicissitudes of the Caledonian and Glasgow & South Western companies up to 1923, when they were united under the umbrella of the grouped London, Midland & Scottish company. Let there be no doubt that the rivalry—which first showed itself in the manoeuvring for official and commercial approval to build a line over the Border—ended with the two lines' eventual completion! Probably the written works of the late D. L. Smith are the best record of the suspicion and mutual contempt with which the two Companies' staffs regarded one another.

One point of interest concerning the Caledonian was its failure to prevent the North British from eventually wresting the accolade of Scotland's biggest railway from the company officially endorsed by the Smith-Barlow commission and given the name *the Caledonian* Railway to perpetuate its 'official', definitive status (a shareholder named McCallum was not contradicted in 1855 when he claimed to have suggested the Company's name when it was first floated).

The North British never matched the 'Caley' for style or elegance—C. Hamilton Ellis once compared a North British train to a rather faded tiger—but the growth of the NBR from the 1860s onwards was as unexpected as it was considerable. Again, it all came down to the Caledonian's failure to absorb the Edinburgh & Glasgow—had they done so (and differences were largely settled between the Companies by the 1850s), it is difficult to envisage the North British becoming a major company in the Scottish railway network. Indeed, a glance at Scottish receipts in the *Railway Times* in the 1850s shows that the NBR came a poor fourth in turnover behind the Caledonian, Edinburgh & Glasgow (the two Companies lumped together for weekly published returns!) and the GSWR. The Edinburgh Company's amalgamation with the E & G in 1865 gave it a pathway to the west, and a foothold in Scotland's largest city.

*     *     *

So let us return to the topography of the Gretna area, where the rails across the Border, formed by the River Sark, had an unusual distinction in railway terms.

After the North British opened a branch to the Caledonian line just south of the latter's Gretna station in 1862, the ¼ mile of the Caledonian tracks over the River Sark was used by all three of the major rail companies in the south of Scotland. (This of course also happened at Carlisle, between the Citadel station and Caldew junction.) The NBR had its own station east of the Caledonian

*Despite having a population of only about 1,000 in the latter half of the nineteenth century, Gretna had no fewer than three stations on public railways. This, the North British terminus of the branch from Longtown, was the third of them. At the time of this photograph, it was probably being administered by the Caledonian Railway for a fee of £37 per annum, shortly before complete closure in 1915. (J. L. Stevenson collection)*

building at Gretna; given the traditionally friendly relations between the GSWR and NBR, only anticipated hostility from the other one of the three companies could have persuaded the North British to build Gretna's *third* station, two of which were not only badly situated for the good people of Gretna, but were in the wrong country.

For the use of the Caledonian's bridge over the Sark, the GSWR and NBR agreed to pay a toll of 4½d (approximately 2p) per passenger, cattle costing 2d more per head. Interestingly, the legislation setting this up, the North British/Edinburgh & Glasgow Amalgamation Act of 1865, specified this as one of three junctions where the NBR and GSWR could exchange traffic, the others being in Glasgow and at Annan. The latter of these two alternatives is a fascinating feature of the story to span the Solway estuary, as the next chapter will disclose.

Traffic between the systems at Gretna was probably fairly light in passenger terms, any thought of promoting a potential Edinburgh-Belfast (via Stranraer) service stillborn by the GSWR's treaty commitments to the Caledonian. (Of course, the NBR also had great hopes of developing Silloth as a port for Irish traffic.) As it was, passenger trains from Longtown called first at the Gretna (NBR) station before reversing out, resuming their south-westwards course and crossing the Caledonian where a stop was made at the main-line station if previously requested by passengers, and then continuing to Gretna Green station of the GSWR. In the opposite direction the stop at the Caledonian station was timetabled. The actual transfer operations took place at Gretna Green station and GSWR green was not seen at Longtown.

In 1910 there were two passenger trains in each direction on the branch, or more correctly, this link between two Companies crossing a third. A Gretna Green resident wishing to travel to Edinburgh could leave the GSWR station at 08.03, spend 32 minutes at Longtown, and be at Waverley by 12.06, in just over 4 hours. But what would be the point of that? By catching the 09.17 Caledonian train, and with no changing, Edinburgh (Princes Street) could be reached at 12.23. As no trains ran on the NBR branch in the afternoons, there was no question of day return traffic being catered for by that route. Indeed, the last passenger train out of Longtown left at 10.32, necessitating a 06.15 departure from Edinburgh on the Waverley Route 'parliamentary', as the legally necessary all-stations service was nicknamed. (If 4 hours or so seems a long time for a 90-100 mile journey, bear in mind that such a trip is not possible by rail nowadays at all.)

There surely would have been scope for the NBR and GSWR to offer a Dumfries-Langholm service with full Edinburgh connections at either Longtown or Riddings. Hospital visits or 'Town Hall' business in Dumfries would always be necessary for Langholm people, as mentioned in the chapter on the Langholm branch, and surely should have been catered for by the GSWR and NBR companies, while also offering an Edinburgh-Dumfries service.

1910's complement of passenger services on the branch—operated until this time almost invariably by a former Edinburgh & Glasgow 0-4-2—was equalled by the number of freight services. There were departures from Longtown at 07.25 and 19.40—the latter coming from Langholm—returning from Gretna at 09.05 and 21.15. The usual goods locomotive in the years before the First World War was No 49, a Drummond 0-6-0 tank named *Gretna*. Interestingly, GSWR 'up' and 'down' directions appeared to have been followed by trains travelling between the systems; the up evening goods from Langholm, for example, changed to a down service at Longtown.

These transfer arrangements—unimaginatively limited though they were in the case of passenger provision—continued until 1915 when war came to the Solway shores. Requiring a flat area for an ammunitions factory, where the buildings had perforce to be isolated from one another, the War Office lighted on the Dornock-Gretna-Longtown area as an ideal site. On 29 July the NBR was informed that its entire Longtown-Gretna branch was being requisitioned, that the connection at the latter end might have to be altered, and that either compensation or reinstatement would be arranged. The NBR lost no time in complying with this order; a printed circular was distributed to staff by 4 August and complete closure came on the 8th.

For the previous seven years the Caledonian had administered the NBR's station for an annual fee of £37 4s 2d (£37.21p), confirming the irrelevance of building such a station in the first place when a friendly company had a perfectly convenient one nearby, and indicating that rolling-stock transfer was the Gretna site's major function. The Caledonian had no objection to the other two companies transferring traffic at Carlisle after extending their traverse of Caledonian metals by some 8¾ miles 'during the period of control'. However, it was made clear that such an arrangement would be strictly 'for the duration'. This would effectively deprive the GSWR and NBR of an exchange junction so, although the GSWR had not received a copy of the War Office order, the two companies petitioned the Railway Executive for reinstatement of the line rather than compensation.

In fact, Gretna South connection appears to have been restored (or possibly not removed at all) before all three companies had lost their separate identities at the Grouping of 1923. Ironically, the allied GSWR and NBR found themselves in different companies, while the sworn enemies of the Caledonian and 'Sou' West' had to settle their differences within the new London, Midland & Scottish company.

Archival records show that early in 1924 the LNER Scottish area staff held a conference to discuss the possible reinstatement of the Gretna connection 'in the position and to the condition in which it existed prior to its being interfered with by the Government' (this despite the fact that rail plans of the time clearly show the connection in existence). The goods department were included in this meeting, but the passenger department protested that they had not been invited, even though the future of the former NBR passenger station was discussed. The excluded department head pointed out that the station's booking-office was already in use as a residential dwelling, and that major investment would be involved to reopen it.

It is doubtful if the LNER ever seriously considered reopening the Longtown-Gretna line to passengers; indeed, the reason for the goods staff being consulted on the future of the tiny Gretna terminus was that freight trains in NBR times used to occupy the platform for vehicle number-checking and for the examination of loads.

By 1923 the LNER Gretna branch was open once again for freight traffic and was worked as a branch from Longtown. Five years later there was only one freight timetabled in each direction (13.00 from Longtown, returning from Gretna at 14.45). Timings were exactly 2 hours later on Thursdays, this skeleton service being operated by a pilot engine from Carlisle. Up and down directions now corresponded with the Waverley Route. Ten years later, there were no trains timetabled at all, the 09.00 Carlisle-Hawick pick-up freight operating the branch as required on its return (unscheduled) journey back from Hawick. The branch, which became part of the connecting network from the Kingmoor marshalling yard in the 1960s with a new connection southwards, served for a time as an up link from the Waverley Route until shortly after the latter's closure in January 1969, but still appeared to have rails intact from the Carlisle direction as far as the Smalmstown area, on the author's last visit, in April 1988.

The Gretna (Caledonian) station was the second to close, when the (north) junction was upgraded in 1951, and the GSWR Gretna

*A unique picture of Gretna's fourth station – Gretna Township – with a train having just arrived conveying the predominantly female workforce back to their living quarters from far-flung parts of the huge munitions complex during the First World War. It was possible for private freight and passenger trains to travel between Dornock (Eastriggs) and Longtown without passing on to a public railway, and crossing the Anglo-Scottish Border by the system's own bridge over the Sark. (J. L. Stevenson collection)*

*The former Caledonian station of Gretna lies reduced to rubble as 'Black Five' No 44672, based at Carlisle (Kingmoor), heads towards that city with a freight from the main line on 6 August 1966. (Douglas Hume)*

Green station followed in 1965. (There is some possibility of its reopening, although ScotRail appear at the time of writing to have made that conditional on new tourist developments taking place in the area.) The GSWR turnout is now singled, nonsensically reducing its value as a diversionary route for Carlisle-Glasgow traffic. On a recent passenger journey on the line, as if to underscore its 'forgotten' character, the guard announced a permanent way slowing at Gretna Green as Annan station—'If leaving the train, please make sure you have all your luggage with you' etc!

The munitions factory already mentioned greatly intensified railway operations in the Gretna/Eastriggs area, and this is dealt with in what greater detail the author can command—given the complex's essentially secretive nature—in an Appendix. It gave Gretna its *fourth* passenger station (at the temporary housing area called Gretna Township south-west of Gretna Green itself; it would surely be a peacetime record for a community of its size, although the area's wartime population was some 20 times greater than normal).

If Gretna Green is connected in the public mind with marriage and romance, there was precious little spirit of conciliation and amity in the first railways to meet there. Nowadays it can be passed by the modern traveller in seconds at high speeds, but its railways history rewards more careful study.

\*       \*       \*

As with the Lamberton crossing on the East Coast line, the 'frontier' nature of Gretna on the West ceased in 1923. The Caledonian and

GSWR companies were grouped together in the London, Midland & Scottish Railway, although not on 1 January as was the case with almost all of Britain's other railways. The Caledonian contested the legality of amalgamation, and this was not finalized until well into the summer.

Grouping began a rationalization of railway facilities in the Carlisle area, as might be expected, while the construction of the Kingmoor marshalling yard in the 1960s transformed the topography of the landscape west of the Carlisle-Gretna main line. To the modern traveller, the marshalling yard, with its acres of rusting rails half-buried in vegetation, and the lines of condemned vehicles, is a sad testimony to the lack of far-sightedness of BR management at the time.

Nowadays, electric-powered trains glide between Carlisle and Gretna in a matter of little more than 6 or 7 minutes, with the newly introduced 'Sprinter' diesel units on the former GSWR services taking not much longer. It is all a far cry from the days when steam engines in the Caledonian's Prussian blue or the magnificent LMS 'Duchess' 'Pacifics' in their crimson lake strove to pass Gretna Junction in 'even time' (9 minutes) from Carlisle.

On the author's last steam-hauled trip northwards across the Border at the Sark Bridge, a 'Jubilee' 4-6-0 fairly tore along the former Caledonian main line, making me wonder about the irony of having travelled ponderously south to Carlisle over the Waverley Route earlier that day behind a diesel locomotive of far greater power. If any proof were still needed that the Caledonian Railway built the fastest rail route between Glasgow or Edinburgh and Carlisle, here it was.

# SOLWAY VIADUCT

## Solway Junction Railway

'The most exciting rail link between Scotland and England'—John Thomas

The Solway Viaduct has never received the attention it deserves from rail historians. Five years in the building, this mile-long structure carried a single track some 35 feet above low water in this deceptively calm estuary. Scottish engineer Sir James Brunlees (1816-1892) designed a low structure of 193 piers, with an average span of 30 feet, requiring the use of nearly 5,000 tons of wrought and cast iron, and with foundations sunk to a depth of 40 feet.

The viaduct was undoubtedly one to seize the imagination, and may have had a seminal effect on British rail history. Dumfriesshire writer Thomas Jackson believed that its construction acted as a spur for the later bridging of the great firths of Tay and Forth. Bearing in mind the fate of the first Tay Bridge, Jackson writes graphically of the courage required by crews working heavy mineral trains across the estuary on dark stormy evenings 'in full knowledge that not far beneath them lay the treacherous waters of the Solway with its fast-flowing tides'.

Although it handled 45,000 tons of ore—its original *raison d'être*—in its first year, and in Edwardian times was crossed by three passenger trains each way per day, the Solway Junction Railway's major construction had an unhappy history. Severe weather conditions dogged the viaduct almost from its opening in 1869-70, and 45 of its supports were demolished by ice-floes in 1881. One such floe was measured at over 240 square feet and was 6 feet thick!

This damage kept the structure out of commission for three years, but an even more chronic problem was the scouring effect of the 12-knot currents on the viaduct's foundations. Large stones had to be tipped into the firth to protect the piers, creating a problem after demolition. This came in 1934-5, passenger services having been withdrawn between Annan (Shawhill) and Brayton from 1 September 1921. Freight traffic had already dwindled because of the cheap availability of imported Spanish ores, and the number of smelting works springing up in West Cumberland.

Even after demolition, the viaduct's site was a problem for its owner since 1923, the London, Midland & Scottish Railway. An artificial reef formed in the estuary where the stones remained after the viaduct piers had been removed or broken off by the demolition contractors. After a number of fishing boats had been damaged, the Board of Trade demanded that the LMS have the stones removed, and this had to be done laboriously by hand, using railway surfacemen equipped with waders, in the years up to the Second World War.

\* \* \*

One evening in August 1864, three men met at No 1 Victoria Street, Westminster, to convene the first Board Meeting of the Solway Junction Railway. They were Alexander Brogden and James Dees, Cumbrian ironmasters, and Charles Tahourdin, the Company's Secretary. Incorporated by an Act of Parliament of 30 June 1864, this railway venture was intended to transport haematite from Cumberland—where its production had increased seven times within the previous seven years—to the iron foundries of Lanarkshire, avoiding the already bustling railway junction of Carlisle by what was, at the time, Europe's longest railway bridge over the hostile waters of the Solway Firth.

On the face of it, their Solway venture seemed unlikely to succeed. Two rail companies were already active on the south shore, the Maryport & Carlisle and its neighbour the North British, the latter

*Rails across the Border – in this case some 35 feet above low water in the Solway Firth which separates Scotland and England. This northward-looking shot shows the watchman's hut positioned about one-third of the way from the English shore to prevent unauthorized crossings on foot. It must have been an unenviable job in winter. (J. J. Cunningham)*

*A Class '47' diesel waits to leave Annan (GSWR) with a Glasgow-Carlisle semi-fast in August 1987, a service now taken over by 'Sprinter' units. The present-day state of Annan station, once described by O. S. Nock and G. Biddle as 'the best surviving early station in south-west Scotland', is a pale shadow of its former self, and its dilapidated platform canopy is particularly noticeable in this photograph. (Author)*

with branches from Carlisle to Port Carlisle and Silloth. On the Scottish shore, the Glasgow & South Western's main line from Carlisle to Glasgow ran through Annan parallel with the shore-line, and the Caledonian's main line between those cities was only a few miles distant.

The SJR's route plans had to be altered almost as soon as they were made, owing to NBR interest in the area. Originally the SJR 'main line' was to run northwards from a triangular junction at Brayton on the Maryport & Carlisle, alongside the NBR Silloth branch for 3 miles, before crossing the Solway between Bowness and Annan. Here, there was to be a spur westwards to the GSWR station, while the main line continued northwards to Kirtlebridge on the Caledonian's Carlisle-Glasgow route. Branches to Annan Waterfoot and Port Carlisle were proposed.

However, the NBR's plan for a line south from Abbey to Leegate complicated the issue, the result being that the Solway company would be given preference provided its line went by Abbey. The Maryport & Carlisle were prepared to be amenable to the new arrival, provided it went no farther south than Brayton, where the Maryport Company agreed to offer exchange facilities.

Possibly the existence of the established Companies in the area acted as a life-saving guarantee for the infant Solway Company, since none of the four railways could afford to assume that its rivals would not invest in the proposed line. As a result, the Company Minutes show considerable interest from other lines, with the NBR prominent initially. The Company's Chairman, Richard Hodgson, personally assured the SJR Directors in the autumn of 1864 that it was not necessary for the new Company to build its track parallel to the NBR in the Abbey Holme area, as had been proposed, since running powers could easily be arranged. Indeed, it was not long before the idea of reciprocal powers for the Edinburgh-based Company over the proposed Solway Viaduct was being mooted, and the NB made tentative enquiries in January 1865 about placing its own staff in the SJR's station planned for Annan. Indeed, the North British/ Edinburgh & Glasgow Amalgamation Act of 1865 actually cites Annan as one of three interchange sites between the NBR and GSWR companies.

It appears that legislation in 1866 gave both these companies the opportunity to contribute up to £100,000 capital in the SJR (presumably between them) and there is some justification for believing that the ultimate operator—the Caledonian—was far from being the obvious partner the new Solway Company was having to seek. Evidence given by the NBR in particular to a later parliamentary committee bitterly pointed out how that company had twice practically assisted the Solway Company (over running powers), but had not even been invited to subscribe in 1867. Apparently the NBR's financial difficulties at that time were so well known that no approach was made to them, while the GSWR decided not to commit capital.

*Solway Junction where the spur from the Solway line met the GSWR main line near the present-day Annan station. At one time this junction was legally specified as a location for the exchange of traffic between the NBR and GSWR, on the assumption that the former company would have running powers over the estuary. All that was in the past as a Midland Compound pilots a former GSWR 4-6-0 southwards towards Carlisle around 1930. (J. J. Cunningham)*

Much was later to be made of the Solway Directors' claim that the line over the estuary was to become 'a common route open to all the Scotch companies with which it was connected'.

A Deviation Act was required before the Junction's route was finalized, and Maryport & Carlisle compliance was assured by the new Company undertaking not to penetrate deeper into the ore-producing area of Cumberland by way of a projected Bromfield-Maryport extension.

The SJR now issued 32,000 shares, with capital of £320,000 and loan capital of £106,000, and had the good sense to appoint James Brunlees as its Engineer. The chairmanship of the new Company was taken by Alexander Brogden, a South Wales ironmaster based at Ulverstone, and he undoubtedly knew of Brunlees's work in building two major viaducts for the Furness line between Carnforth and Ulverstone. The longer of these was the 1,200-feet Leven Viaduct—the Solway Viaduct would have to be four times as long!

Brunlees (Sir James after 1886) is undeservedly little known today although his career was a triumph for a self-educated Victorian professional. Son of a Kelso gardener, he had been forced to leave school at 12, but showed great mathematical skills, and was soon helping Alexander Adie, a surveyor friend of his father, in planning estate roads near his home town. Careful saving allowed him to study at Edinburgh University and he found work on the Bolton & Preston Railway (later part of the Lancashire & Yorkshire) and on Locke's staff in constructing the Caledonian main line north of Carlisle. At the time of his Solway appointment, Brunlees appears also to have been designing the 16-acre Avonmouth dock, and he was later knighted for his work on the Mersey rail tunnel. It is not perhaps too surprising to learn that he also designed and built seaside piers around the country, including the 1¼-mile Southend pier. The Solway Viaduct was not perhaps far removed from such constructions! Interestingly, this much-underrated Scot was also engineer to the Channel Tunnel Company from 1872-86, in conjunction with Sir John Hawkshaw. Obviously, the Solway Junction Company had chosen a good man for the job at hand.

Brunlees accepted an offered fee of £8,000 'in satisfaction for his services and disbursements of himself and his staff', although half of this impressive sum was made up of shares in the as yet unconstructed railway. With Waring Brothers and Eckersley appointed as contractors, work on the new viaduct began in the summer of 1865, the site of the structure being chosen, one writer (Dr A. Earnshaw) believes, because of its particular stability. This was the course of the Stonewath, a ford which followed a moraine left by a retreating glacier. But Brunlees soon had a major problem to face concerning the bridge's design.

Even as the foundations were being driven using gimlet-pointed piles, a controversy had begun as to whether the bridge should have a swing span to allow marine traffic through. In September 1864 the Board of Trade shocked the SJR by asking for a 60-foot span opening section to be incorporated. Brunlees pointed out that this would require a movable section no less than 150 feet long (60 on each side of a pivotal area), that this was 50 per cent longer than had been required for other estuarine waterways, and would be a nightmare to operate in winter conditions. Brunlees argued cogently that the NBR's proposed running powers from the south to a possible harbour at Annan Waterfoot would reduce the need for river traffic going up

*So underused was this great estuarine viaduct that it is almost impossible to trace genuine photographs of a train crossing the Solway. This picture shows the lengthy structure when still in use, or shortly after closure, looking southwards from the Seafield Farm area on the Scottish shore. (J. J. Cunningham)*

to Port Carlisle, particularly since that Company had filled in the canal from there to the city of Carlisle.

Probably unknown to the SJR Directors, the NBR had been considering closing Port Carlisle Harbour in July 1862, while investing in the development of nearby Silloth. On the other hand, the Board of Trade could hardly take it on itself to write off Port Carlisle as a viable harbour—there had been a twice-weekly steamer sailing from there to Annan and Liverpool in the mid-1850s—so the SJR Directors authorized Brunlees to leave an 81-foot gap in the structure until the matter was resolved. This they decided to expedite by persuading Port Carlisle residents to admit that their harbour had no commercial future anyway! One wonders how they set about this!

Meanwhile, another problem—shortage of capital—caused work on the viaduct to be suspended in August 1866 (ironically, probably the best construction period of the year) while loans on debenture were awaited. A modern examination of the Company's files also reveals yet another complication; the SJR had not troubled to observe the niceties of securing the right to build a viaduct over the Solway in the first place, and the resulting suspicion is reinforced by cross-referring to the archives of the Crown Commissioners (as they were then) for Her Majesty's Woods, Forests and Land Revenues.

This source suggests that the viaduct was being built quite illegally on someone else's land! Access from the foreshore on the Scottish (or 'Scotch' as it was known then) shore to mid-channel was agreed to be sold to the railway company for £105, and this amount was fixed by the Commissioners in July 1865. When the sum was still unpaid the following May—and we can surmise that the infant company was in no hurry to pay any of its bills—the SJR's legal agents answered the Commissioners' reminder by disingenuously suggesting that they had assumed that they would have to wait for the resolution of the question of who owned the intended site of the southern half of the vast structure. This was not an entirely unreasonable attitude to take, given the complex question of the ownerships of the English foreshore and seabed to mid-channel. At that time, the 2nd Earl Lonsdale, Lord Lieutenant of Cumberland, claimed ownership, and the railway Company did not legally obtain their necessary clearance until 1878, for an undisclosed sum. Later correspondence shows that the Commissioners conceded the Lonsdale claim to the foreshore but not the seabed.

Effectively the SJR completed a railway on land whose ownership was disputed on one side of the firth, and commenced building when legal matters were not finalized on either side. Indeed, after agreeing to pay £105 for the Scottish land purchase, the Company then appears to have lost the Banker's order sent to it for signature; the money was not deposited until 1 March 1867.

However, the future may have looked a little brighter by October 1866 when the NBR sealed a memorandum to the Board of Trade confirming its belief that no opening section was necessary in the new viaduct. This may have been the time when the major rail concerns started to take a serious interest in the SJR, possibly realizing how damaging a rival's interest in the struggling infant Company could be. The NBR, as already noted, helped in the Junction Company's dealings with the Board, and must still have envisaged a role for itself in south-west Scotland—even if it had to approach the area through another country!

Inevitably, this drew Caledonian interest; the Glasgow Company had just lost out to the NBR in the latter's rather surprising amalgamation with the Edinburgh & Glasgow. This may well have prompted the CR offer of agreement to the Solway Directors on 22 March 1867, one which must have guaranteed the new Company's immediate future; £60,000 of shares were to be purchased by the Caledonian, with full CR representation on the SJR board. If there was any spark of interest from the nearby Glasgow & South Western in the new cross-frontier venture, it is not visible in the Minutes; possibly the GSWR had its hands full at the time with its proposed merger with the Midland, an enterprise which Parliament was to disallow in July 1867.

May 1867 saw the drawing up of an agreement between the SJR and the Port Carlisle Railway & Dock Company, by which the latter agreed not to oppose then current SJR legislation in the House of Lords, and to back the latter Company's insistence that a swing-bridge was unnecessary. The price of this compliance was the Solway Company's undertaking to accept the NBR's lease of the Port Carlisle Railway at a fixed rent of £3,500 if the NB pulled out of the existing agreement. This may have been a gamble by the SJR, at a time when there must have been considerable wheeling and dealing not strictly detectable in the Board Minutes, but at least the bogey of an opening section in Europe's longest bridge was disappearing, and indeed the Board of Trade appear to have been satisfied.

Despite this advance, it was at this time, June 1867, that the SJR's former chairman, James Dees, tendered his resignation as a Director on the grounds of ill health. But the Board was having none of it. The resignation was refused, the Directors trusting that Mr Dees's health 'may soon be re-established, and he will be able to co-operate with them in the completion of the undertaking'. Faint hearts would not see the Solway bridged! (Dees was another self-taught engineer who made a personal fortune in haematite mining, and had by this time virtually retired on the proceeds. His obituary records that he suffered from gout, dying in 1875 at the age of 60).

No sooner had the Company overcome one financial hurdle when another was erected in its path. In September of that year the SJR's contractor demanded compensation for the failure of the Company to authorize the construction of the Port Carlisle and Waterfoot branches, respectively south-east and north-west of the viaduct site. No less than £24,000 (in shares) was awarded to the contractor although, in the absence of preparatory earthworks, it is difficult to see how

such compensation could be justified. This month also saw the Caledonian appoint Colonel Salkeld as their representative Director and the Solway Company's new backers inspected the progress of construction.

With a sudden burst of optimism, the Directors ordered the Viaduct's design to have bays and embankments suitable for double track, but on the English side only. This seems puzzling, particularly since doubling was considered some 18 months previously, and was deferred at a Board Meeting in February 1866 owing to the additional cost of £20,000, not including the cost of extra track and alterations to any necessary swing-bridge. Why in late 1867 it should be thought desirable or necessary to have provision for double track, and at the south end only, is unaccountable. This extra width is believed to have extended to the first 200 feet or so at the southern end of the viaduct, according to the recollections of a visitor shortly before demolition. The approach embankments, still to be seen today, were faced with pitching for 479 yards on the west side of the Scottish shore and 164 yards on the east side, while the English embankment was pitched for 460 yards on each side.

Gradually, the Solway's unpredictable tides and bores were bridged, and in early 1869 the SJR's directors found that they had more or less a railway. This was despite the difficulties encountered in crossing the 2 miles of Bowness Moss, south of the viaduct, where the contractors were often having to dig 50 feet before finding a firm foundation. Indeed, this natural obstacle was to cause more of a

*Abbey Junction, where the SJR left the North British Silloth Branch and struck southwards to Brayton. This 1931 view is looking in the Carlisle direction, over a section of Silloth line where the SJR held running powers. When the Solway line opened, so poor were the receipts that the company's directors had to pay a proportion of the running powers' costs from their own pockets. (LRGP)*

construction problem than the viaduct itself, and the section of line was soon to fail a Board of Trade inspection. It was decided, somewhat late in the day (spring 1869), to give Bowness a passenger station following the presentation of a petition from local residents. Meanwhile, other parts of the line were being readied for trains, there being a farcical episode in March 1869 when the signalling contractor put up signals before his contract was agreed.

Running powers over the North British branch between Kirkbride and Abbey Junctions (which effectively isolated the Abbey-Brayton section of the SJR) were concluded on 4 September 1869, to apply from the 13th of the month. But more importantly, an agreement was drawn up in Glasgow on the 1st between the Solway and its northern backer. This concerned what is described as the 'temporary' working of the SJR by the Caledonian, under the agreement of 22 March 1867. How temporary this was supposed to be is not immediately clear, but what is beyond doubt is that the Caledonian would effectively operate the Solway Junction trains, while maintaining the SJR's nominally independent status.

From 14 September 1869, the SJR would 'run' its services with CR staff paid for by the smaller Company, and using two locomotives loaned by the Caledonian 'to be maintained in good order by and at the expense of the SJR'. The signalling at the northern end of the line, at Kirtlebridge, was to be arranged to the Caledonian's satisfaction at 50-50 cost between the Companies. The locomotives were based at a depot here, on what is now the West Coast Main Line, although the archival files show that an engine-shed also existed at Brayton, certainly in the mid-1880s.

An interesting sidelight on locomotive workings on the Solway Junction is one writer's insistence that Neilson of Glasgow delivered four locomotives, two 0-6-0s and two 0-4-2 tanks, for service on the line around 1868. These bore works numbers 1388/9 and 1217/8 and CR running numbers 542/3 and 540/1 respectively. This author is unable to confirm this information; the Board Minutes appear to contain no locomotive orders, and the Neilson order-book shows the latter two works numbers applying to 0-4-2 tender engines with the Caledonian specified as customer (the records are presumably correct although understood to have been rewritten in the 1930s). Indeed, apart from an order for station seats in 1870, there is significantly little in the way of railway administration details in the SJR ledgers, suggesting that either the archival records dealing with such matters are missing, or that the Caledonian simply got on with it.

But this is to anticipate. Colonel Elland of the Board of Trade inspected the line on 4 and 5 November 1869, passing it for freight traffic, although this is not specifically stated in the records. But there was no such outcome for a later BoT inspection on 2 June 1870, when the Inspector refused to pass the Bowness Moss section for passengers. Despite this setback, passenger trains traversed the length of the line between Kirtlebridge and Brayton by August of that

**Above left** *Kirtlebridge, the northern terminus of the Solway Junction Railway. Although this shot, looking northwards, is pre-Second World War, the track in the branch platform on the left has already been lifted. (J. L. Stevenson collection)*

**Left** *Brayton Junction with the line to Abbey leaving the Maryport & Carlisle main line beyond the signalbox. This was effectively the southern terminus of the Solway Junction line, losing its service northwards in 1921. (LRGP)*

**Above** *Bowness-on-Solway station, looking towards the viaduct in the 1900s. The construction of the station was something of an afterthought for the SJR's directors, but must have been popular with local inhabitants, who were infuriated by the delay in reopening the viaduct after it was damaged in 1881. (J. L. Stevenson collection)*

year. The Solway Junction was in business—but only just.

Excursion traffic featured prominently in the early months of operation, with the good people of Cumberland being invited to sample the delights of Dumfries (the long way round, via Lockerbie), and disappointingly few Beattock citizens being transported to Keswick. The fact that only four days' notice was given of the latter excursion underlines the inexperience of the SJR administrators, while, in contrast, the actual rail operations—carried out with Caledonian know-how—appear to have gone comparatively smoothly.

By 1880 it was possible for a rail traveller to leave Edinburgh at 2.25 in the afternoon (or 2.15 pm from Glasgow) and, after changing at Kirtlebridge, be in Bowness by 5.56 pm. There was a total of 11 up and 10 down traffic movements throughout the whole line including short workings, with three passenger trains and one mixed in each direction. In addition to the main stations, Whitrigg, on the Bowness Moss, was operated as a 'flag' station. Here the gateman would signal trains to stop if required; passengers wishing to alight had to inform the guard at Bowness on up journeys and at Abbey on down trains.

The GSWR seems to have been slow to realize that the 'wooden horse' of the SJR contained Caledonian enemies who now reached into 'Sou' West' territory at Annan as well as Dumfries. Not surprisingly, relations between the GSWR and SJR took a downward turn with the former refusing to accept passenger specials over the

Solway Junction spur at Annan in September 1870—perhaps with good reason, since the records suggest that this 32-chain connection was not passed for passenger traffic by the Board of Trade until 2 August 1872.

Nor were financial problems very far away. In August 1870 the NBR's £1,250 fee for running powers at Abbey Holme was paid half by the Caledonian, while the other half had to come from the pockets of the SJR Directors themselves, so inadequate were receipts. Within a year the Secretary was taking it on himself not to bank what receipts there were 'in consequence of the trouble likely to arise from a seizure of the Company's monies by creditors' as the Minutes record the matter with brutal frankness.

Smelter construction in the West Cumberland area increased in the years 1868-71, undermining the *raison d'etre* for the viaduct even before it opened. The problem was not helped by the GSWR's insistence of routeing traffic between south-west Scotland and Cumberland—particularly fireclay being transported from Kilmarnock to Whitehaven—via Carlisle, even when senders' labels specified travel over the viaduct.

There was no choice for the new company. At a time when it could scarcely afford litigation, it was going to have to take the GSWR to court.

This case dragged on for around 18 months, with the SJR attempting to obtain an interdict (a Scottish injunction) against the GSWR's rerouteing practice. This they failed to do, failing again on appeal. By 1872 we find the railway Company operating under the protection of the Court of Chancery, and contemplating the drastic step of selling the northern section of its line, Kirtlebridge-Annan, to the Caledonian. Obviously, failure to reach traffic targets was crippling the Company, so it is not surprising that the sale of the northern section went through on 30 September 1873. The Caledonian paid £86,439 for the line as far south as Annan (Shawhill) station, in which the SJR retained a half-share.

Within a few years the Solway Directors began to wish that they had managed to sell off the rest of the railway. For in January 1881 severe winter conditions produced polar-like ice on the estuary and the viaduct was damaged by, of all things, ice-floes, not a meteorological phenomenon normally expected in Britain. Forty-five piers and 37 girders collapsed, one of the bombarding ice-floes being measured at 27 yards square and 6 feet thick, allegedly putting the viaduct's watchmen to undignified flight. No train crossed the Solway for another three years.

It was not engineering difficulties which made this hiatus last so long, more the fact that the structure's collapse questioned the whole reason for the line's existence. The Company's Minute Book for the period reveals the most extraordinary procession of events taking place in the next 3½ years. The SJR would have three different Chairmen, two of whom would resign, a state of war with the Caledonian would break out—both in the Boardroom and in court—a new Act of Parliament would be necessary, contractors would fail and the Company's own engineer would step in to save the day. His reward would be a pay cut! Meanwhile, the traffic, such as it was, went elsewhere.

The saga began at Carlisle Citadel station on 8 February 1881. A SJR Board Meeting was held there (at 8.30 in the morning) to hear a report from the firm's engineer, John Brown, of the newly inflicted damage, along with his estimate that repairs would cost £18,000. This was calculated 'on the assumption that the fallen girders are not seriously damaged, a point which cannot at present be ascertained'. (Nor would it be for at least 2½ years, during which time the metalwork lay where it had fallen in the Solway.)

It is perfectly evident from the Minutes that the Solway Company had been unable or unwilling to obtain insurance cover against such damage as had occurred. Indeed, when receiving another estimate for repairs of £23,239 from James Brunlees, the viaduct's designer acting as consultant engineer, the Minutes frankly recorded that 'This company has no funds available for the purpose of reconstruction'.

Not surprisingly, it was immediately decided to ascertain the Caledonian's view of the crisis. This proved to be easier said than done, the Directors recording in March their 'regret that the Caledonian Railway Company directors have neither been able to meet them at the time suggested nor appointed any other time'. This was an ominous sign that the Glasgow Company may well have felt that its junior partner was not perhaps worth the trouble and expense envisaged, and the Solway Directors must have been deeply worried men. Their Secretary, possibly in response to a request from the

Caledonian, records that 'The Solway Directors are not prepared to submit in writing their views as to the future of this Company but [believe] that the interests of the two Companies are so many and varied that it is essential that an early interview should be held'.

On 27 April 1881 the SJR Directors offered the railway for sale to the Caledonian but received only a verbal negative reply, one which they asked to be communicated in writing. It was, and the Caledonian seemed equally unmoved by petitions received from citizens in Bowness and Annan requesting reconstruction of the viaduct. The relevant Caledonian Minute records somewhat baldly: 'resolved to decline to find money for rebuilding Bridge and to repeat the demand of this Company [ie the Caledonian] to have the Bridge rebuilt; also to decline the proposal for purchase—the terms not being satisfactory'. If the hapless Solway Directors had any lingering hopes of Caledonian assistance these must have died once and for all when, holding a Board Meeting at the Victoria Chambers, Westminster, they learned that 'the Caledonian people are not in Town'.

By July, the Company's visionary founder and chairman, Alexander Brogden, had resigned, the relevant Minute recording the Board's acceptance of this with regret and mentioning 'his long continued . . . on behalf of the Company'. The space was later filled in with the word 'energy', as if it had taken some time to think of something! His successor was W. B. Page; Brogden himself was to die tragically in a domestic accident in 1892.

The following month saw the Caledonian demand 'compensation' for the SJR's failure to reconstruct the viaduct, although it is difficult to believe that the larger Company imagined that they could recover any or all of their investment from a Company whose disastrous financial affairs they were in a perfectly good position to know about. On 20 September, Messrs Page, Dees and Tahourdin were admitted to a Caledonian Board Meeting. This conference does not seem to have resolved anything, the Glasgow Company demanding an independent engineer's report and estimate. John Strain, consulting engineer, was soon invited to visit the viaduct, where he produced photographs, two of which are included here. His fee was £206 12s 4d, paid nearly a year later.

From the outset of the crisis, the North British, under the expansionist managerial control of John Walker, had offered to assist in working the SJR's traffic through Carlisle, although this was not apparently taken up. But as the autumn began to draw on, the increasingly desperate Directors must have considered closer links with the NBR. At the beginning of November 1881 an advert was placed in the *Carlisle Patriot* (this newspaper was specified particularly) publicizing the company's intention of floating a new shares issue not only to repair the viaduct but also to build a line to Port Carlisle (one of its earliest intentions). From there running powers would be applied for to Carlisle itself; in return the NBR would be offered running powers southwards to Brayton—which would represent their

**Above** *The Solway Viaduct, viewed from the English shore, stretches northward into the mist of 1 November 1881. Note the barrier at the viaduct's entrance.* (Scottish Record Office)

**Right** *Like some grisly momento of the first Tay Bridge, a single rail dangles over the deceptively calm waters of the Solway. These two photographs were taken by engineer John Strain, commissioned by the Caledonian and LNWR companies to assess the extent of the ice-induced damage. The width of the structure at this point suggests that it was designed for double track although the additional cost prevented the whole structure from being so designated.* (Scottish Record Office)

southernmost incursion into England—'*and any other points of the Company's railways*'. In case the Caledonian did not take the hint, there would also be an appraisal of the Caledonian's working agreement.

War with the Caledonian started at about this time. The larger Company opposed the SJR's parliamentary initiative to improve its financial position; for one thing, the 1867 agreement between the Companies prohibited the SJR creating further share issues without Caledonian written consent. Following a SJR shareholders' meeting, an action committee was set up which apparently had an amicable relationship with the Directors. Indeed, in January 1882, following the resignation of Chairman W. B. Page, one of their number became the new Chairman. Page resigned because he was no longer a shareholder. Before leaving he suggested 'some alterations' in the Minutes, a request which the Directors ignored, preferring the Secretary's version of what appears to have been a fairly murky episode. The new Chairman was John Musgrave of Whitehaven.

While hoping for a new financial base, in July 1882 the SJR considered four tenders for repairs to the viaduct, fully 18 months after their line was effectively cut in two. These varied from £24-26,000, the Company accepting the cheapest, that of Messrs Dixon and Thorne, although some requirements of the Board of Trade prevented sealing the contract before September.

The Solway Junction's half-yearly reports as published in the *Railway Times* give little hint of the turmoil in the Boardroom. A small profit was being reported regularly during this period, the traffic diversions being 'in a manner perhaps as convenient to the public, and about as profitable to their own company', as the magazine put it ambivalently.

From this point on, the Solway Company appears to be fighting on two fronts, struggling to repair its viaduct in the teeth of Caledonian opposition. The latter Company's actions may appear in retrospect to be negative and obstructionist, but the 'Caley' Directors—'adopting the new-fashioned doctrine of opposing their landlords' as the *Railway Times* commented—may reasonably have seen the SJR's manoeuvrings to raise capital by attaining access to Carlisle over North British metals as scant reward for the Caledonian's interventions of 1867 which ensured that the Solway would be bridged.

Relations with the Caledonian reached rock bottom early in 1883. When Major Andrew Green Thompson, the larger Company's representative on the Solway Board, attempted to enter three Board meetings at Whitehaven in February and March, his presence was objected to by Chairman Musgrave. Thompson claimed to have received intimation of the meetings from the Company Secretary, and he is marked as 'present', despite his unhappy reception. It appears that the Caledonian's £60,000 worth of shares had been transferred to him and another Director personally, presumably to enable at least one of them to insist on attending SJR Board Meetings.

However, within six months the Chairman was again contesting the Caledonian's right to be represented at Board Meetings, although his hostility was more understandable on this occasion since the Caledonian had by now served an interim interdict on the SJR Secretary to prevent him paying for the costs of the Company's new legislation out of the capital account. Interestingly, this decision was reversed on the SJR's appeal and costs awarded against the Caledonian.

The product of all this activity was the Solway Junction Railway Act of 1882, giving the company wide borrowing and fund-raising powers. A 1¾ mile line south-eastwards from the viaduct to Port Carlisle was empowered to be built, but only after the viaduct was reopened for traffic, while running powers were to be awarded (it appears, although the Act is scarcely a paradigm of lucidity) for the SJR from Abbey Junction beyond Kirkbride Junction to the NBR's junction with the NER at Canal Junction, Carlisle, although not apparently from Port Carlisle. In return, the NBR appeared to be awarded similar powers to Brayton, which if taken up, would have represented the most south-westerly appearance of North British gamboge. These running power arrangements were to lapse if not put into effect within five years.

The smaller Company also won another victory over its former ally the following summer. In July 1884 the House of Lords favoured the SJR against the Caledonian in the latter's continuing opposition to the Solway amending legislation, and the Glasgow Company had again to pay all costs. The 1882 Act had specifically protected the Caledonian's interest in the SJR, thus weakening any protest from that Company, who were apparently trying to force the Solway Company to accept £30,000 worth of debenture stock.

But this is to anticipate, for by 1883 the SJR was contemplating an extension south to Braithwaite on the Cockermouth, Keswick and Penrith line, yet the fallen girders were still on the seabed—a disgraceful monument to overweening commercial vanity. Matters could not have been helped by gales in January 1884, which caused damage to the approach embankments, but meanwhile something had gone seriously wrong with the chosen contractors.

In mid-February 1884 consulting engineers Brunlees and McKerrow gave a report on unfinished works and on 31 March the Directors were officially told that their own engineer, John Brown, 'has been engaged in completing works contracted for by Dixon and Thorne', costs being charged to the contractors. Accounts appeared before the Directors for the purchase of hardware materials, and, lo and behold, by 22 May Major Marindin of the Board of Trade passed the repairs as being satisfactory. Unless the SJR records are inaccurate on this point, it appears that goods trains had already been using the viaduct for some five weeks by that time, with passenger services resuming on 1 May! The *Railway Times* announced that 'the structure is of much stronger construction, having flanges which, it is anticipated, will break any ice floes'.

Relations with the Caledonian had continued at a low ebb, despite a SJR appeal for a conference in February 1884. In October the Chairman was once again objecting to the presence of Thompson (now promoted to Colonel), although one Board Minute records that, hostile or not, the other Company was to time a connection out of Brayton to connect with the 7.55 ex-Whitehaven. Obviously the Caledonian was honouring its agreement to carry on services, operating the line during the viaduct's severance as separate branches from Kirtlebridge to Annan and from Bowness to Kirkbride. The northern section had seven up and nine down train movements timetabled, while Bowness had four mixed trains daily southwards (but two of the northbound trains were empty vehicle workings). The SJR Directors learned that, despite some difficulty in publicizing timetables, 'traffic is improving somewhat'.

This proved too optimistic, however. On 27 November the faithful Brown was told that 'in face of the poor traffic his salary would have to be reduced or his services dispensed with'. At a meeting the following Christmas Eve it was decided, apparently at Brown's initiative, that his salary would be settled at £150 pa 'but with no use of Sand, Slopes or Gardens hereafter'. The arcane nature of this contract is equalled only by its meanness. Secretary Tahourdin, who had served the Company since before a yard of track was laid, had his salary reduced by one-quarter, to £300 per annum.

Given the perilous nature of the SJR's central cord across one of Britain's most dangerous estuaries (in January 1886 Brown reported the recurrence of ice!), plus its wrangles with the Caledonian and the GSWR, the main surprise about the line is the fact that it appears to have retained its independence until as late as 1895. On 1 July of that year, it (on paper at any rate) amalgamated with the Caledonian, although the SJR remained in existence to meet certain legal requirements until the Grouping in 1923.

\* \* \*

By 1910, a year when Britain's railways achieved their zenith in terms of prosperity, the Solway Viaduct was being crossed by only three passenger trains each way per day, making a nonsense of the vast investment. The Maryport & Carlisle Railway made less than a commendable effort to offer connections to and from Maryport at Brayton. Passengers arriving from Scotland had to wait 53, 26 or 21 minutes before connecting with southbound trains, but there were shorter waiting periods of 20, 10 or 5 minutes northbound.

Frustratingly little has been recorded about railway operations over the Solway. One historical source records that even the Caledonian's biggest outside-cylinder 4-6-0s traversed the Viaduct, suggesting that there were no clearance or weight problems. 'The Solway Viaduct is only intended for the running of Vehicles not bringing [bearing?] on any one span more than 1½ tons per lineal foot,' the Appendix to the 1885 Caledonian working timetables decreed. The Board of Trade

*Bromfield, an intermediate
station on the Abbey-Brayton
section. By 1910 only three trains
stopped here daily in each
direction, plus a single Brayton-
Abbey working once a week.*
(LRGP)

*Bromfield, an intermediate station on the Abbey-Brayton section. By 1910 only three trains stopped here daily in each direction, plus a single Brayton-Abbey working once a week. (LRGP)*

had insisted on a 20 mph speed limit after reopening in 1884 (there had been a similar speed limit before the 1881 accident; interestingly, there was at that time an even more severe slowing to 10 mph, on part of the Bowness Moss section).

Obviously the local passenger service would not merit the attention of large engines, and it was reported that around 1905 an 'Oban Bogie' (a Brittain 4-4-0 design) and a 'small train of black stock' sufficed to meet passenger needs.

Written accounts of train journeys across the Solway are few and far between. The only first-hand memory of crossing the Solway by rail comes from Sylvia Thompson of Bowness who recalls a child-hood crossing: 'There was a high tide and it felt like being on a ship at sea, a most exciting journey'. Older Cumbrian children were apparently sent across the estuary to Annan Academy in the years before closure.

Mr H. M. Liddell of Fairford told *Backtrack* magazine in 1988 of a northbound crossing made by his father at the turn of the century:

'My father ... had a very clear memory of one journey to Annan in a glass-ended observation carriage which was coupled to the locomotive. This was four-coupled with inclined outside cylinders, and he had a good view of it as it was running tender first. The weather was stormy, which made for an exciting crossing and probably a very wet one for the engine crew. Presumably the engine was an elderly survivor of Connor's 2-4-0s . . .'

Up to 50 goods wagons per train could be worked across the Solway depending on the type of engine power used, although, perhaps significantly, the line is not included in the Caledonian's table of mineral loadings. At the time of reopening, the line came under the authority of a traffic inspector based in Edinburgh and a permanent way inspector in Carlisle! The nearest breakdown crane was at Carlisle (Etterby), and standing arrangements existed for it to reach the line via the Maryport & Carlisle for speed's sake (although a similar arrangement over the GSWR to Solway Junction would surely have been at least as quick). Operations on the line in 1885 were worked as follows:

| | | |
|---|---|---|
| Kirtlebridge-Annan | - | Train Staff and a red ticket |
| Annan-Bowness | - | Train Staff and blue ticket |
| Bowness-Kirkbride | - | Train Staff and yellow ticket |
| Kirkbride-Abbey | - | Block Telegraph |
| Abbey-Brayton | - | Train Staff and green ticket |

The Company's Directors still met at least once annually until the end of the line's theoretically independent history, the viaduct's closure in 1921 not even being formally notified to the Board! At the time of Grouping, the SJR's business address was Sandown, Isle of Wight, the Company being amalgamated with the LMS as an independent body. The Solway Directors each received £150 compensation, the official documents recording that the Caledonian was then paying an annuity of £4,500 to operate the line. Those railway historians interested in company law may care to note that, although the Solway Junction was 'grouped' on 1 January 1923, the Caledonian retained its separate existence for a further six months. But this was only one facet of the story of the Solway Junction Railway, one of the most curious rail enterprises in the history of either of the countries it brought physically together.

\*          \*          \*

Closure of the viaduct to passenger trains in 1921 applied equally to freight. The LMS records show that 31 August 1921 was effectively

*Kirkbride Junction, where the Solway Junction line from the north joined the NBR Carlisle-Silloth branch. This view, looking westwards in 1931, shows that the connection had been restored at the LMS's request, to facilitate demolition operations on the viaduct, although this may have proved unnecessary as commercial contractors were used. (LRGP)*

the closure date altogether 'owing to the Solway Viaduct becoming defective and the traffic not justifying the heavy expenditure necessary'. The connection with the LNER at Kirkbride Junction was removed in 1927, although the LMS refused to allow the relevant signals and signal box fittings to be removed, and the lifting of track between there and Bowness was not authorized until October 1936. The LMS Scottish Committee Minute Book shows that this was done with a profit to the company of some £2,054. By this time the viaduct itself was gone, one of the largest civil engineering constructions to vanish from Britain's landscape.

Why nearly 15 years passed between its closure and removal is not entirely clear. In October 1930 the LMS asked the LNER to reinstate the Kirkbride connection so that the track could be retrieved as far as milepost 8 at Bowness. The cost was calculated at £159, including running powers for 20 ballast train workings over a three-week period. There was obviously no question of the materials being retrieved by working these trains over the viaduct itself and using Annan's sidings and facilities. Having attained this southern point of access, the LMS did not make use of it at that time; indeed, the LNER was still enquiring in 1932 as to when the LMS would begin track-lifting, only to be told that 'we do not consider it advisable at the present time to proceed with the demolition of the viaduct'. Precisely why is not at all clear. The LNER files reveal, however, that their Area Engineer saw the closure of the LMS's Abbey-Brayton section as an opportunity to upgrade the former place's siding accommodation with the LMS unconsciously helping to defray the cost!

Local author Thomas Jackson believed that pressure from the Solway Navigation Commissioners eventually moved the LMS to face up to the question of the structure's future. Whatever their motivation, it was soon to become evident that the railway Company could hardly be blamed for postponing the demolition job for as long as possible! The saga of the viaduct's removal is chronicled in detail in Scottish Record Office archives, and makes engrossing reading.

Although supposedly barricaded at both ends at this time, the viaduct acted as an unofficial walkway between Scotland and England. The more liberal licensing laws on the English side resulted in thirsty Scots crossing the Firth to slake their thirsts on Sundays, particularly since this area of Dumfriesshire was under state licensing. This had been introduced in the First World War, when workers in the new munition plants near Gretna and Dornock found little other than alcohol on which to spend their unexpectedly high wages. Curbs on the sale of liquor were quickly introduced and remained in force for a surprisingly long period into our own times.

One shudders to think of how Scottish imbibers fared on their journey back from Bowness, crossing a semi-derelict structure, probably in darkness. The author's relatives frequently made unofficial crossings of the viaduct—although not in search of alcoholic

*A walker's-eye-view of the Solway Viaduct, looking south. This picture was probably taken after closure but before a barricade was erected to try (unsuccessfully) to prevent illicit crossings of the Firth. Note in the foreground the distant signal lacking the usual chevron; the line's signals were erected before a contract had been finalized. The placing of the signal gave warning to northbound trains before encountering the junction with the spur to the GSWR line south-east of Annan. (J. J. Cunningham)*

refreshment, or so they insist!—and they still remember the gaps in the rotting superstructure giving a glimpse of the racing currents below. One can only suspect that the LMS was being more than a little casual in their lack of determination to remove the viaduct—or at the very least render it inaccessible—and this air of casualness was to persist throughout the whole demolition saga.

Demolition certainly seems to have been considered in 1929, not long after the Kirkbride connection had been severed, and this involved the LMS Divisional Engineer, based in Glasgow, memoing the Company's Scottish solicitor to enquire if the Crown Commissioners, owners of the foreshore, would have to be informed of any move to demolish. This being confirmed, another delay resulted and it was not until March 1933 that more positive steps were taken.

On 30 March of that year, Divisional Engineer A. H. McMurdo advised the Solicitor's department that demolition was soon to proceed and that the Crown Commissioners should be informed. This was done on 5 April, proving to be of almost academic interest to the Commissioners, as it was not until the following August that they informed the Company that they were unaffected by the move. However, by that time the LMS had received an unexpected letter on the matter.

The Crown Commissioners were perhaps not interested in the

viaduct's fate, but the Board of Trade certainly was. Alerted by the Commission, the Board's Mercantile Marine Department made an intervention that, to the historian at least—for the 1930s railway staff were probably unaware of it—strangely echoes the Board of Trade's insistence in 1864 that the interests of riverside communities upstream should be considered. On 12 April 1933 the Mercantile Marine Department enquired if 'complete removal is intended' and whether 'all the piles will be drawn'—obviously, the Solway's commercial and fishing interests were not being forgotten by the Board.

When passed on to the Glasgow-based McMurdo, the Board's enquiry drew the fairly casual response that the manner of demolition would be 'left pretty much with the contractor'. The engineer went on to say that the embankments, consisting of 'pitching with heavy blocks of stone which are in very good condition' would not be touched. In a further letter on 22 June, McMurdo made the fateful remark that, where the viaduct's piles could not be removed altogether, they would be broken off 5 feet 'below the level of the firth'.

In contrast to the LMS's apparently easy-going attitude to problems involved in, and consequent to, the demolishing of the viaduct, the Board asked for a report from its Coastguard Superintendent based at Hoylake, a Mr Pennington Legh. His report was commendably detailed, even estimating the number of fishing-boats active in the estuary—30-40 on the Scottish side, each 'half-decked' vessels of 4 tons displacement and drawing 3 to 4 feet of water, with eight or nine similar boats operated out of Silloth. As if to echo the SJR Directors of nearly 70 years before, he reported that mercantile traffic to Port Carlisle was 'done away with' and was unlikely to return following demolition. The Coastguard's comments regarding potential danger from partially removed viaduct supports to fishing vessels and, indirectly, to stationary stake-nets, were remarkably prescient. The Board was undoubtedly better informed at this stage than was the LMS.

'Having caused local inquiries to be made,' the Board of Trade ominously informed the LMS on 4 August, 'we understand that stone ballast was tipped between and around the piles of this structure and . . . this has become firmly set with mussels, weeds, etc.' The letter went on to speculate that an 8-knot tide meeting freshet conditions (ie an increased volume of water coming down the estuary from swollen rivers) might redistribute boulders loosened by those piles which could be removed, thus dangerously exposing those which could not, and creating a navigational hazard. Not surprisingly the Board insisted that 'Every effort shall be made during the course of demolition to withdraw the piles completely'. Other matters raised were the need for permission for any temporary structures below high-water mark and for adequate warning notices to be posted in neighbouring towns and villages.

Six days later the Board formally gave permission for demolition to take place, subject to these conditions being observed. It is a measure of the LMS office-bearers' offhand approach to the whole subject that they had not even apparently realized that such permission was required in the first place.

It was already too late in the year for work on the viaduct to be started, as a contractor had still to be appointed. By 8 May 1934 this had been effected, the Company Solicitor being informed that Arnott Young Ltd of Glasgow would begin demolishing the superstructure above the high water mark on the 14th. Despite the imminence of the starting date, the solicitor was asked to prepare warning notices to inform the public of these operations, and this led to a fairly testy exchange between McMurdo and James Wilson, the solicitor, the latter reasonably pointing out that there was hardly sufficient time for this within the six days specified. Not too surprisingly, Arnott Young had to be told to delay commencing operations until the end of the month while posters and newspaper advertisements were prepared, these having to be sanctioned from Euston.

Work to remove one of Britain's most imposing civil engineering constructions got under way at last, but the LMS's problems were only about to begin. On 21 June 1934 the Board of Trade's Mercantile Marine Department reported to the railway company that

'three lines of stumps are left projecting about eighteen inches to two feet from the bed of the Firth, each stump having from four to six rugged bolts about four inches long protruding vertically from the top ... this must constitute a serious danger to boats navigating the Firth in the vicinity.'

The Board specifically requested that the piles should be removed as soon as the superstructure was dismantled immediately above.

McMurdo informed Wilson that the offending stumps were being removed by winches on board a dredger, his reassurances being tempered by his statement that the contractor was trying to obtain a bigger dredger, indicating a certain lack of confidence. When told that the Board was still demanding a statement on the matter, he admitted that 'trouble' was being encountered and that other methods of removal were being attempted. His advice to Wilson that the removal of the upper part of the structure would not precede that of the foundations 'to an unreasonable extent' provoked a demand from the latter for this phrase to be explained.

Meanwhile the Board wrote again, objecting to 'two sections of pile stumps *about ten feet high* about fifty yards apart, left standing'. Not only that, but extracted stumps were being left on the foreshore, where a high tide might hide them from fishermen or even bathers. It all seems so casual, the contractor perhaps being lax in thinking that his employers were well out of his way some 100 miles to the north, although, to be fair, the difficulties of the job should not be underestimated.

Around this time a fatal accident occurred involving the drowning of three workers, two of them contractor's employees, the third being William Adam, an LMS joiner. In March of the following year the railway company paid £600 compensation (plus £2 10s (£2.50) 'court expenses') to the Adam family, promptly claiming it back from Arnott Young, probably since the accident happened on a boat belonging to that company.

The problem complained about by the Board in August 1934 was presumably dealt with, as there does not appear to have been another official intervention until June 1935. This time the Board demanded the removal of the hull of a wrecked lighter—possibly involved in the fatal accident—and more remaining stumps, while pointing out that a line of stones and boulders was now visible at low water. When pressed on this last matter by Wilson, McMurdo pointed out, on 27 June, that their removal was not covered by Arnott Young's contract. Faced with this omission, Wilson waited for more positive action from the Engineer, replying to further Board hastening enquiries in August and September with the request for 'a day or two' to look into the problem, but the time interval requested quickly passed. The Board pressed again on 4 October, prompting the unfortunate lawyer to reply desperately, 'I regret the delay here. It, however, does not lie with me.' He even warned McMurdo that very day that he had informed the Board of Trade about the latter's apparent tardiness— the archival files do not contain any reply from the Engineer to this seeming lack of diplomacy.

Pressure continued to build up on the LMS in what was fast turning into a bungled episode—ironically, at a time when the viaduct itself had now been demolished. The Board then passed on a letter, dated 7 October, from the Secretary of the Annan Fishermen's Association complaining that the stones originally tipped into the estuary to protect the foundations were now 'standing up like a pier' at low tide. Not only were these expected to be a danger to navigation but might deflect currents from their normal courses, with all that might involve for the net-fishing industry. It was, he concluded, 'a disgraceful business'.

The LMS's Chief Officer in Scotland, James Ballantyne, now entered the fray, possibly as the result of a complaint by McMurdo or Wilson about the other. Ballantyne assured the solicitor that McMurdo was estimating the cost of removing the offending boulders—but this was nearly four months after it became obvious that Arnott Young would not remove them under the existing contract! When, on 9 November, the Board of Trade demanded that action be taken on the removal of the boulders and wrecked lighter *within 14 days*, Wilson almost disassociated himself from his company's behaviour on the matter. He also pointed out to Ballantyne that the problem of the stones, first discussed some 17 months earlier, was still no nearer resolution; any fisherman damaging his boat in the area of the erstwhile viaduct would have a legal claim on the LMS. Ballantyne replied reassuringly, explaining that experiments were to be made using explosives to solve the problem. But still the Board pressed for action, demanding a statement of proposals *by return of post*. This was on 27 November, to which Ballantyne suggested to Wilson that he forward details of the explosives experiments, although the files do not appear to contain a copy of any such reply.

Whether the LMS had replied or not, the Board of Trade now brought in its legal department. On 18 December the Board's lawyers requested an assurance by the following Monday that action would begin to have the obstacles removed. The LMS was very close to finding itself in court.

More hand-wringing from Wilson resulted in letters on 19 and 23 December, desperately assuring his counterparts at the Board of Trade that the contractor was being asked to remove the wreck of his boat, and that explosives were to be used to disperse the unwanted reef. Not too surprisingly, this brought forth the reply that explosions might only succeed in dispersing the stones, thus increasing the danger to boats from uncharted obstacles.

Asked for an opinion on this, McMurdo insisted that explosives would reduce the height of the reef and that individual stones loosened would sink in the sand. However, he admitted that no trial explosions had yet taken place (this was mid-January 1936), owing to unfavourable weather in the area. When this advice was communicated to the Board it asked for all explosive work to be done by 25 February, so as not to interfere with the opening of the salmon season. Had the LMS, in planning the use of dynamite, realized that the Solway is an estuary famed for its salmon-fishing by the use of standing shore-nets? One can almost rest assured that it had not.

Fourteen days before the 'deadline' for an end to explosive demolition, only one successful blast had been achieved. This seemed to convince the LMS Chief Officer that the two weeks remaining would be sufficient, an opinion that appears not to have been based on tidal information, never mind any knowledge of the weather conditions that could prevail when a winter wind came off the Irish Sea! How much blasting took place within the next two weeks is not clear from the files, but by 17 March the Board informed the LMS that the salmon-fishing interests did not regard these demolition methods as a threat to their livelihood. To employ an appropriate phrase, the company was 'off the hook'. But the problem of the reef remained, local opinion being that sand was rapidly building up.

The Company's officers now decided, somewhat belatedly, to see the site for themselves. No sooner had the Chief Officer, District Engineer and Solicitor of the LMS arranged to travel to Annan by the 09.30 out of St Enoch, when the plan had to be changed because of other commitments. In any event it appeared that they had not realized that their visit to the Dumfriesshire foreshore would have to coincide with low-water—much later in the day—and an afternoon visit was finally arranged for 4 May 1936. They then found a sandbank covering the offending reef to a depth of 4 feet, giving no immediate cause for concern, and returned to Glasgow on the 18.26 from Annan. But this turned out to be little more than a rehearsal for

*Apart from the embankments, the only vestige that remains of the once mighty Solway viaduct is this set of piers on the English shore, photographed in September 1985. This section of the viaduct was wide enough for a double track, a facility which is believed to have extended for a short distance on the southern end only; the SJR found that it could not afford to accommodate two lines throughout the length of the structure.* (J. L. Stevenson)

a more serious site visit on the 20th, made at the request of the Board of Trade.

On this second occasion the Company's unfortunate Engineer found himself in a group whose visit was ordered by the Board, the official representative being Captain Brandon RN. Fisheries interests were present in the form of a Mr Menzies from the Fisheries Board for Scotland, as well as local fishing representatives.

The Solway at low tide on the 20th showed yet another changed aspect to its visitors, with the main river channel running to the south of the former site of the watchman's hut on the viaduct (approximately one-third of the way from the English shore), while no northern channel was visible, a pond having formed in its usual course. As it happened, not a stone or rock was to be seen, and the party's members agreed that nothing need be, or indeed could be, done, unless or until such rocks showed themselves again. Nevertheless, one of the local fishermen gave the LMS's man, Mr McMurdo, a difficult time, insisting that the latter acknowledge his firm's culpability in the matter, something which McMurdo declined even to discuss. In this he was supported by Captain Brandon, and the Engineer's report on the visit described the atmosphere as 'pleasant'. Brandon even produced an 1837 chart which showed a major sandbank running east and west parallel with the Scottish shore.

Just over a fortnight later Wilson received an assurance from the Board that no further action need be taken on the matter unless the stones were exposed again. He was to enjoy nearly a month's peace of mind!

'I thought that this matter was ended.' This was the despairing reaction of James Wilson, the LMS solicitor, when he received fresh ill-tidings from the Solway in mid-July 1936. An Annan-based fisherman named Wilfred Woodman had been sailing past the former site of the viaduct some 700 yards from the Scottish shore when a 4-foot hole was torn in his boat's timbers by an underwater obstacle. Only vigorous baling, he claimed, had saved his life and that of his crewman; £10 compensation was immediately demanded.

But when one of McMurdo's assistants stared out over the estuary from the Annan side on 6 August, not a rock was visible, the problem area being covered to an estimated depth of 5 feet by sand. The company's Marine Superintendent was also brought in for an opinion, which was that buoying the danger site was not practicable; indeed, during the month of August the main channel was reported to be moving northwards almost daily, exposing new stones as it went.

The Marine Superintendent summarized the problem:

'I am of the opinion that there will be continuous trouble over the stones with every shift of the Channel and suggest that some arrangement be made with a local fisherman that whenever the stones show, stakes are put in to mark the place and the Coy. informed, so that steps can be taken to remove the top stones to a sufficient depth.'

It was a belated outburst of common sense, to harness local knowledge to help eradicate the problem, especially since McMurdo's department had now worked out that only 'a few hours of work' on the stones would be possible in each month. McMurdo added, in a memo to Ballantyne, 'This work will be of a recurring nature, and it will not be possible to say how much will have to be done or when the work will be finished'. In other words, the LMS was beginning at last to see the nettle to be grasped.

The late summer and autumn of 1936 saw up to 40 lengthmen— railway track workers—being employed to stand in the middle of the estuary breaking up the offending boulders whenever local fishermen advised the LMS of a period of favourable tides approaching. It was an unpleasant task for the men, in an area notorious for quicksand and where the incoming bore could travel faster than a man could walk. The wages expended by the LMS came to £15 per day and more compensation had to be handed over in the following November when another boat—this time ferrying railway employees—was damaged by another unseen obstacle: £5 15s (£5.75) was paid by the LMS without argument.

By the end of the year the problem seems to have been overcome. The LMS and some of its most senior officials in Scotland could return to the business of running a railway. The Solway Viaduct, the most westerly of the railways crossing the Anglo-Scottish Border, was no more.

# APPENDIX

# The eighth crossing

The introduction to this book mentions seven sites where Britain's railways crossed the Anglo-Scottish Border. There was in fact an *eighth* location, just west of the Caledonian Railway's Sark Bridge, shared with the GSWR and North British Companies. This was part of the military munitions complex developed between Dornock (Eastriggs) and Longtown, sprawling through the Gretna Green area during the First World War.

Because of its military nature, the history of this private network is not easy to research; indeed, the site of the private rail bridge over the Sark is even difficult to find, the current Ordnance Survey map showing only an embankment on the western side—one which could easily be mistaken for a flood dyke. West of this point was Gretna's *fourth* passenger station, known as Gretna Township (see p123-4), and serving the temporary housing complex for munition workers.

At one time military traffic could be transported by private standard gauge line all the way from Dornock to Longtown, via an underbridge just south of Gretna (CR) station. This joined the NBR's Longtown-Gretna branch at Dornock junction ('to be disused,' says a NBR plan of January 1922) on the east side of the West Coast Main Line, and the branch then continued as double line eastwards to Longtown. An idea of the size of the Ministry rail network can be gained from the fact that the private engine-shed near Longtown had no fewer than three roads.

A large 2-foot gauge network also existed, although details are understandably sparse. Details of the locomotives of both standard and narrow gauge systems are given in the *Handbook* (Section N) of the Industrial Locomotive Society.

Peat workings north and north-east of Gretna spawned their own narrow gauge systems, the rails in the Mill Hill area still visibly embedded in the minor road off the A6071.

# BIBLIOGRAPHY & SOURCES

Coleman, Terry. *The Railway Navvies* (Hutchinson, 1965)

Dow, George. *The First Railway across the Border* (LNER, 1946)

Elliot, John J. *The Border Railways - their growth and decline* (MA Dissertation, University of Edinburgh, 1969)

Ellis, C. H. *The North British Railway* (Ian Allan, 1955)

Hillman, Mayer and Whalley, Anne. *The Social Consequences of Rail Closures* (Policy Studies Institute, 1980)

McCartney, R. B. *The Railway to Langholm* (In press: details from the author at "Cairndhu", Walter Street, Langholm)

Mullay, A. J. *The Railway Race to Scotland, 1901* (Moorfoot, 1987)

Nock, O. S. *Main lines Across the Border* (Nelson, 1960)

Peacock, Bill. *Border Country Railways* (Cheviot Press, 1982)

Robertson, C. J. A. *The origins of the Scottish railway system, 1722-1844* (Edinburgh: John Donald, 1983)

Stobbs, A. W. *Memories of the LNER, Rural Northumberland* (Penrith, nd)

Thomas, J. *The North British Railway*, Vols 1 & 2 (David & Charles)
———— *Regional History of Railways of Great Britain*, Vol 6 'Scotland: Lowlands and Borders'

Whishaw, Francis. *Whishaw's Railways of Great Britain and Ireland* (1840 and 1842 editions)

White, H. P. *Forgotten Railways* (David & Charles, 1986)

Archival sources relating to the Caledonian; North British; Glasgow, Dumfries & Carlisle; Border Counties; and Solway Junction Railways, and the Crown Estate Commissioners, have been examined in the Scottish Record Office, whose staff are thanked for their helpfulness. Edinburgh University is also thanked for permission to quote from the Elliot thesis.

The author also gratefully acknowledges the assistance of staff at the National Library of Scotland, Edinburgh City Libraries, and the Mitchell Library, Glasgow.

# RAILWAYS ACROSS THE BORDER
## Circa 1914

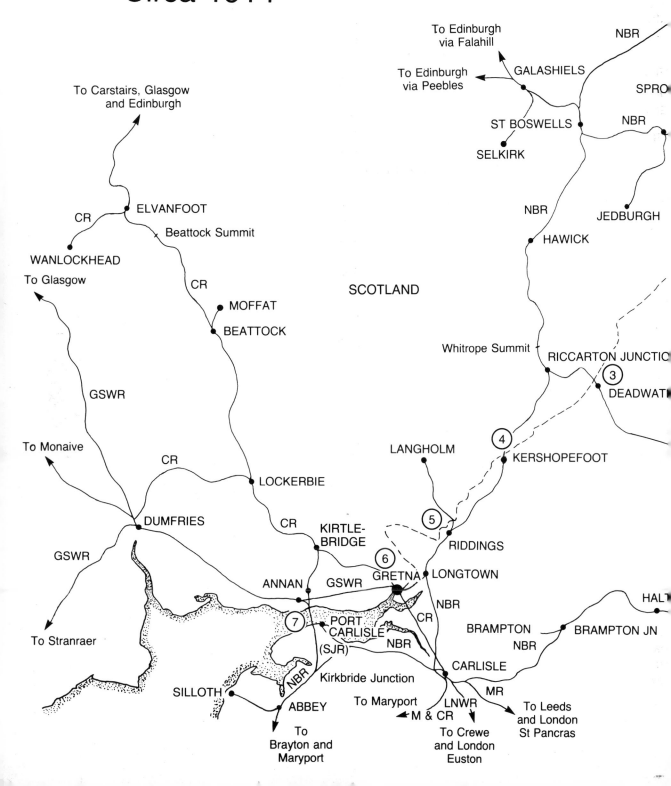

To Edinburgh via Falahill

To Edinburgh via Peebles

NBR

SPRO

GALASHIELS

ST BOSWELLS

SELKIRK

NBR

NBR

JEDBURGH

To Carstairs, Glasgow and Edinburgh

CR

ELVANFOOT

Beattock Summit

WANLOCKHEAD

To Glasgow

CR

MOFFAT

BEATTOCK

SCOTLAND

NBR

HAWICK

Whitrope Summit

RICCARTON JUNCTIC

③

DEADWAT

GSWR

To Monaive

LANGHOLM

④

KERSHOPEFOOT

CR

LOCKERBIE

CR

KIRTLE-BRIDGE

⑤

RIDDINGS

DUMFRIES

GSWR

⑥

GRETNA

LONGTOWN

GSWR

ANNAN

NBR

CR

HAL

BRAMPTON

NBR

BRAMPTON JN

To Stranraer

⑦

PORT CARLISLE
(SJR)

NBR

CARLISLE

MR

SILLOTH

NBR

Kirkbride Junction

To Maryport

LNWR

To Leeds and London St Pancras

ABBEY

M & CR

To Brayton and Maryport

To Crewe and London Euston

# INDEX